Think BETTER Write BETTER

Rob Jenkins

GEORGIA STATE UNIVERSITY

Kendall Hunt
publishing company

TABLE OF CONTENTS

Introduction 1

CHAPTER 1: Why I Wrote This Book—and Why You Shoud Read It 3

CHAPTER 2: Critical Thinking: What It Is and What It Isn't 7

CHAPTER 3: How to Think Critically 17

CHAPTER 4: Some Practical Applications of Critical Thinking 29

CHAPTER 5: What It Means to Write Well—and Why You Should Care 39

CHAPTER 6: The Writing Process 47

CHAPTER 7: Avoiding Common Grammatical Mistakes (That Even the Pros Make) 57

CHAPTER 8: Developing an Engaging Style 73

CHAPTER 9: Making (and Winning) Arguments 91

CHAPTER 10: Using Logic and Reason 113

CHAPTER 11: Writing with Sources 133

CHAPTER 12: Writing Effective E-mails 147

INTRODUCTION

This book is intended as a short, easy-to-read tutorial on making effective written arguments. That begins with clear thinking and carries over into clear writing—hence the title. This book is not meant to be an exhaustive treatment of topics like logic, grammar, or the writing process. Dozens of wonderful books and articles have been written on all those topics, many of which I draw upon and reference in this book. In particular, weighty tomes have been penned on topics to which I devote only a short chapter, like using logic. If you wish to expand your knowledge and further improve your writing and thinking skills, I highly recommend that you read as many of those works as you can get your hands on.

My purpose, rather, is to summarize those topics in a way that is both meaningful and accessible, aimed especially at the majority of readers who have not been and likely will not be exposed to those other, more thorough treatments. In other words, I'm not assuming that you've read any of those other books on writing and thinking, or that you ever will read them (even though you should), so I'm trying to condense the information in a way you can understand and benefit from in practical ways. Admittedly, I leave some things out and just touch on others briefly. Some might criticize me for not spending more time on this or that concept. Okay. I accept those criticisms. I made this a short book on purpose, because I want people to actually read it. There's no way I can say everything there is to say about writing and thinking in 170 or so pages, nor have I tried. I just hope readers take away what I believe are the most important concepts, the ones I believe will help them most in their professional lives.

Which brings me to my next point: This is not an academic book, even though it's designed, in part, as a college textbook. I actually have two audiences in mind: first-year college students, who I want to make sure are exposed to these ideas, and people who graduated from college with ever being exposed to them (or at least, it didn't take at the time) but who now recognize the need to improve their reasoning, writing, and arguing skills. My impression is that the latter category includes a significant percentage of professionals in this country, so I'm hopeful the book will have wide appeal. And by the way, it wasn't difficult to write for a dual audience, because the things I want my students to know are exactly the same things I tell professionals in a workshop setting.

I acknowledge that, in talking about these concepts, I often put my own spin on them. I also, on occasion, avoid technical or academic terminology, choosing instead to explain things in my own way—the way that has worked well with students for over thirty years. So even if you've encountered some of these concepts before, you might find that I'm talking about them in very different ways from what you're used to. Some readers (and especially some of my colleagues) might occasionally take issue with my perspective, and that's fine. As I said, you can always read other books on the topic to get a fuller and more nuanced understanding. For the purposes of this book, I'm far more interested in practice than theory.

Not that I'm unfamiliar with the theory. My graduate degree is actually in rhetoric and writing, and I keep up to date by reading books and articles in my field and attending writing and teaching conferences on a regular basis. (In fact, I read so much on the topics of thinking and writing that, while I was working on this book, I constantly found myself going back and adding something I'd just come across. Eventually, I had to make myself stop doing that, or else this project would have gotten completely out of hand.)

But I'm also a professional writer and editor. In addition to knowing the theories about writing, I also have a pretty good grasp of what actually works on the page—and it's not always the same as what the theories say. Moreover, I've been a college administrator, which is to say a middle manager, for more than half my career. And while leading an academic department might be different in some ways from managing a unit in a large corporation, in other important ways the jobs are very similar. In particular, both require highly developed communication skills and the ability to persuade people effectively. Those two things are what this book is all about, and I have a lot of experience with both—in the classroom and beyond.

Finally, as I mentioned above, I've had over thirty years of practice in teaching people about these concepts—not just college students, but also adult professionals in the higher education, corporate, and nonprofit sectors. As an industry consultant and trainer, I've worked with faculty and staff, mid-level managers, CEO's, rank-and-file employees, hospital administrators, and many others to help them improve their thinking and writing skills. Those experiences have reinforced, for me, the impression that many people who ought to have gotten this stuff in college didn't, for whatever reason. My mission in life is to rectify that situation, whether on the front end with my college students or down the road with adult learners.

WHY I WROTE THIS BOOK—AND WHY YOU SHOULD READ IT

What if college doesn't work the way it's supposed to anymore? I know—that's a strange way to start a book aimed at college students and recent graduates. But stay with me.

Sure, it still works pretty well, in the way that matters most to most people: enabling them to get a good job and make a decent living. (I'm going to stop short of saying "preparing them," for reasons we'll talk about in a moment.) But even that is less true than it used to be. Recent studies show that as many as a quarter of college graduates are underemployed, meaning their earnings don't theoretically match their education level. Moreover, as important as it is to be able to get a good job and make a good living, that shouldn't be the only purpose of going to college, or the only outcome of earning a degree. Ideally, a college education should mean more than that.

Think of it this way. Most people who go to college in this country attend state-supported institutions, meaning taxpayers in that state (and, to an extent, throughout the country) pay a percentage of the cost for them to attend. (That's why private schools cost so much more—because, unless they have financial aid, students and their families have to foot the entire bill.) So why would hard-working residents of a state, many of them without college degrees or high-paying jobs themselves, voluntarily (through voting for state leaders) pay taxes to help people they don't even know go to college? What is it they expect from those people once they graduate? What is it they expect from the state's colleges and universities?

Yes, part of what they want to is to grow the state's economy and increase the tax base by producing more residents qualified for high-paying jobs. That attracts industry to the region, adds revenue to the state's coffers, and generally makes life a little better for everyone. But that isn't all they expect. They also assume college-educated people will be thoughtful citizens, informed voters, and community leaders. That's the real "bang" they get for their buck.

Unfortunately, there's plenty of evidence that both groups of "consumers"—the taxpayers who help fund colleges and the businesses that hire their graduates—are becoming increasingly dissatisfied with the product. Nationwide, state support for higher education has declined significantly over the last decade or so. (Although it has edged back up slightly in recent years.) I suppose we could blame the Great Recession, or do what most people do and mark it down to "mean-spirited," "anti-education" state legislators. But that last explanation doesn't really wash, since most of those legislators are highly educated themselves, and they no doubt, like all parents, want their kids to get a good education. Perhaps a better explanation is that the people they represent, the taxpayers in their districts, are no longer certain that colleges are using public money wisely and doing what they were designed to do.

Certainly the businesses that hire new graduates seem to feel that way. Study after study, over the last ten years, shows that are employers are increasingly ambivalent about the quality of college graduates—and the institutions that produce them. Overall, they report that colleges are doing an okay but not a great job, and they have some specific, major complaints. Namely, they say that the recent college graduates they're hiring for their companies are lacking in two key areas: communication skills (specifically, writing) and critical thinking.

This issue sort of exploded (at least, in the higher ed world) back in 2011, with the publication of the bombshell book *Academically Adrift: Limited Learning on College Campuses*, by education professors Richard Arum and Josipa Roksa. Using surveys and assessments, Arum and Roksa studied over 2,300 traditional-age students at twenty-four colleges and universities across the country, many of them highly selective. The results were shocking, to say the least. According to their findings, forty-five percent of those students "did not demonstrate any significant improvement in learning" during their first two years, and thirty-six percent showed little to no improvement over the entire four years. They also found that students tended to do better, especially in the key area of writing and critical thinking, when their courses required more reading and writing, and that liberal arts majors tended to fare better in those areas than students majoring in other fields.

What does it say about most college courses, and most majors, when about a third of all students apparently learn little or nothing during their four years of college—especially when it appears that they're not learning how to think and communicate like educated adults? Why would taxpayers want to fund that? Why would companies hire them?

In the years since 2011, Arum's and Roksa's methodologies have been criticized and their findings disputed by other scholars. Unfortunately, the corporate world seems to agree with their conclusions. Even before *Academically Adrift* was published, back in 2010, the highly respected higher education consulting firm Noel-Levitz surveyed nine hundred employers nationwide, asking them about the performance of the recent college graduates they'd hired. The employers identified writing and critical thinking as the academic skills with the "largest negative gap between performance satisfaction and expectation." In other words, of all the abilities they expected new hires to have acquired in college, but were disappointed to find that they lacked, writing and critical thinking topped the list.

Similarly, a 2013 study of over seven hundred employers nationwide, conducted for *The Chronicle of Higher Education*, found that "when it comes to the skills most needed by employers, job candidates are lacking most in written and oral communication skills, adaptability and managing multiple priorities, and making decisions and problem solving." Note that those last four items all fall under the general heading of "critical thinking." The *Chronicle* study also found that "employers place the responsibility on colleges to prepare graduates in written and oral communication skills." Clearly, they are failing in that responsibility, at least to some extent, for reasons we will examine in subsequent chapters. But it's interesting to note that employers *expect* people to learn those things in college, and are disappointed when they don't.

At some point, I wouldn't be surprised to see corporations start taking matters into their own hands and providing training courses for employees to enhance their writing and thinking abilities. But when that begins to happen on a large scale—I believe it's already happening, to some degree—what will that mean for the future of college? Will people still need a college "education," if the colleges aren't teaching them what they need to know, anyway, and the corporations decide they can do better? And in the meantime, consider the benefits to those who already know how to write and think critically—who took advantage of the opportunities afforded them in college or after college to develop those skills (because those opportunities are certainly there). Remember the old proverb: "In the land of the blind, the one-eyed man is king."

But I digress. Another study, this one conducted in 2014 by The Association of American Colleges and Universities, found that "employers . . . give students very low grades on nearly all of the seventeen learning outcomes explored in the study"—and that certainly includes both writing and critical thinking. (Interestingly, that study also noted that students "judge themselves to be far better prepared for post-college success than do employers." So much for the high "self-esteem," everybody-gets-a-trophy mentality.) And finally, in 2016, two large, employment-focused Web sites, Payscale and Future Workplace, teamed up to survey over 76,000 managers and executives in this country—and found that sixty percent of them said new college graduates lack critical thinking skills. Sixty percent!

I don't know about you, but that sounds pretty conclusive to me. (It also sounds like things have actually gotten worse, not better, since *Academically Adrift* was published.) Clearly, as far as the end-users are concerned—the companies that are providing jobs for college graduates, the very jobs they go to college to qualify for in the first place—American higher education is not doing a stellar job of preparing people for today's workplace. And the issues are not technology or globalism or diversity or any of those other "modern" concerns. Instead, they are the same skills that have been necessary for people to survive and thrive and conduct commerce since the beginning of time: the ability to communicate effectively with others and the ability to solve problems using reason and logic.

Those are the skills I am going to be talking about in this book. They are not, by the way, entirely separate or distinct. Rather, they are closely related, complementary skills that work together in myriad ways, many of which we will explore in the following chapters. For now, suffice it to say that one cannot be a clear writer without first being a clear thinker, which is why I'm going to cover critical thinking first. But it's also true that there's little point in being a great thinker if you're not able to communicate those ideas clearly to others. The two work hand in hand.

Your role, as reader, student, and learner, is to take advantage of this opportunity to acquire those skills you will need down the road, and perhaps need right now, the skills employers obviously expect you to have and most professors would also be thrilled to see. However uninteresting you may find the subject matter, you must realize that you do indeed have a vested interest in mastering it—that, to put it bluntly, being able to write and reason well will pay off. Added to whatever other technical skills you manage to acquire, or have acquired, those two abilities will distinguish you from your peers, opening doors for employment and advancement throughout your career. They will also equip you to be a better neighbor, a better leader, and a better citizen, which is also an important consideration, if a secondary one for the purposes of this book.

So to sum up very briefly my answers to the questions posed in the title of this chapter, I wrote this book because there are some things you need to know about writing and critical thinking that, quite frankly, I'm not confident you have learned or are going to learn anyplace else. And you should read it because you really do need to know those things, whether you realize it or not, and knowing them will make your life better in countless ways. Whether you're a current college student being exposed to these concepts for the first time or a recent (or not-so-recent) college graduate who didn't quite get them (or weren't taught them) the first time around, I invite you to read carefully, to really think about what you're reading, and to consider how it might apply to your own life and career. You'll be glad you did.

REFERENCES

Arum, Richard and Josipa Roksa, *Academically Adrift: Limited Learning on College Campuses*. Chicago: U of Chicago Press, 2011.

Employer Satisfaction Survey, *Ruffalonl.com*, Ruffalo Noel Levitz, 2010.

"The Employment Mismatch," *chronicle.com*, *The Chronicle of Higher Education*, March 4, 2013.

"Falling Short," *aacu.org*, *Association of American Colleges and Universities*, December 2014.

"Leveling Up: How to Win in the Skills Economy," *payscale.com*, *Payscale*, May 17, 2016.

CRITICAL THINKING: WHAT IT IS AND WHAT IT ISN'T

What should be the purpose of a college education? I would argue that its primary purpose should be, not to prepare students for any particular career—that's a secondary concern—but to prepare them for adult and professional life after college; to enable them take their place among their fellow citizens as productive members of society; to teach them how to think for themselves so they will indeed be citizens and not mere subjects. For me, that has always been the primary distinguishing feature of an educated person: the ability to think for themselves and not be manipulated by advertisers, politicians, and other assorted hucksters.

The label we attach to this cognitive activity is "critical thinking." Unfortunately, that term has been used (and abused) so much over the last couple of decades that it has become kind of a cliché, a buzz-phrase. As a result, it has, like most buzz-phrases, practically ceased to mean anything in particular. That's especially true in our education system. Get any group of teachers together, from any grade level, kindergarten through graduate school, toss out the question, "What can we do to help students learn better?" and someone in the room is bound to say, "I know! Let's teach critical thinking!" Then someone else will say, "Yes! That's good! Put that on the list." And everyone will nod sagely and stroke their chins, and whoever is taking notes will write it down, and it will go into a report that no one will ever read, and nothing will actually get done and nothing will change. As a professional educator for well over thirty years, I have seen that scenario acted out time and time again.

That's not to suggest critical thinking is not a real thing. Even though the term has been used to the point where it has almost ceased to have meaning for most people, including the people using it, that doesn't mean it doesn't mean anything. It does, and that meaning is crucial, both for individuals and for society.

So what exactly is critical thinking? Simply put, it is the ability to solve problems using logic and reason. It requires us to consider information objectively; to identify and analyze the relevant factors; to recognize and, when necessary, set aside our feelings; and, ultimately, to ask the right questions.

At the risk of stating the obvious, critical thinking actually has two distinct components: first, it requires thinking, and second, it's critical. I'd like to examine both—but first, let's take a moment to consider a little history.

A Little History

The roots of what we now call "critical thinking" can be traced back to the Ionian city-state of Miletus, in the sixth century BC. Philosophers in that city devised a process they called "critical reasoning," by which they meant formulating, proposing, and examining hypotheses. It was very much like today's "scientific method," which is something we don't normally associate with philosophy. The Milesians, however—just like serious philosophers today—shared a common goal with scientists: the pursuit of truth. (Keep in mind that the Latin root of our word "science" means "to know.")

For the Milesians, hypotheses were attempts to explain the nature and origins of the universe. What made their approach unique, however, was the principle of *falsification*—basically, the belief that a hypothesis is not really valid unless someone can argue *against* it. It must be able to be tested. As you know if you've taken any science courses, falsification is still a key principle in the hard sciences (and the social sciences, too, although perhaps to a lesser degree).

Just as an aside, that's why the term "settled science," which we hear thrown around a lot these days, is a complete misnomer. There's no such thing. Science, by its very nature, is not settled. Not only is it always open to debate, but it MUST be open to debate. A scientific hypothesis must by definition be falsifiable in order to be a valid hypothesis. Once something is truly settled, science ceases to study it. We don't, for instance, have groups of scientists currently seeking to determine whether or not the earth rotates on its axis. We know that. Science has moved on to other questions—things we don't know but are trying to find out.

All of this can be traced back to the Milesians, whose ideas gave rise to the great Greek and Roman philosophers along with the famous scientists and thinkers of the Enlightenment and the Age of Reason—in other words, to virtually all the noteworthy advances in science and the arts over the last 2,500 years. And that is where the modern notion of critical thinking comes from—or my definition of it, at least, which I believe is the classical definition. Critical thinking is all about asking questions, pursuing answers, debating ideas openly and honestly. It's about using our brains, our powers of reasoning, to find the truth—or as close to it as we can humanly come to it, at least.

Which brings me back to my two-part definition of critical thinking that I mentioned earlier.

Critical Thinking Means Thinking

Often lost in all the educational blather about critical thinking is the fact that it is in fact a form of thinking—the highest form, I would argue. This is important to understand because, contrary to what you might assume, we as human beings are not necessarily pre-disposed to use our brains any more than we have to. That's especially true of modern human beings in technologically advanced societies. We've created an entire culture that caters to our desire not to have to think too much—about what we're going to eat for dinner, what entertainment we're going to consume, or even where we're going. We have drive-through restaurants, micro-wavable meals, satellite television, and Internet-streaming services. We don't even have to know how to get to one of those restaurants. We can just ask Siri.

This is the world that most of today's college students and recent graduates are accustomed to. (And I have to admit—I'm starting to kind of like it, myself.) I'm not saying it's altogether a bad thing. I'm not opposed to time- or effort-saving technologies. Theoretically, they ought to free up our minds to grapple with other, weightier matters than what we're going to eat or watch on TV. Unfortunately, what tends to happen instead is that we've become so used to having everything handed to us on a figurative platter, we get annoyed when we actually have to think about stuff.

Yet it is absolutely necessary that we learn to engage our brains, if we're going to be productive and successful. In our personal and professional lives, there will be many questions that Siri won't be able to answer, and Googling will only take us so far. We have to think. We have to discipline ourselves to think, because it doesn't really come naturally.

Training versus education. In one of those employer surveys I mentioned in Chapter 1, respondents had the opportunity to add comments. I'll never forget how one hiring manager from a Fortune 500 company explained why he rated new hires so low in the category of critical thinking. He said (and I'm paraphrasing slightly here), "When we hire these young people fresh out of school, many with MBA's, they are thoroughly trained in all the latest theories and techniques. And as long as the situations they encounter on the job mirror the situations they stud-ied in their textbooks, they do fine. But inevitably, something will come up that wasn't in the textbook, and then they have to think for themselves. That's when they become lost."

Among other things, this statement highlights an important distinction between education and training. We often use those terms interchangeably, but they are not the same thing. In fact, although they are clearly related, they are in another sense exact opposites. Training involves conditioning people to know what to do without having to spend an inordinate amount of time thinking about it, something that is necessary in virtually every profession. Think about police officers, who in live-shooter drills are presented with plywood cutouts of different "targets." But one is a woman carrying a baby, while another is a guy pointing a gun at them. They have to learn to react immediately—to shoot the bad guy and not shoot the woman with the baby. If they are not thoroughly trained to respond properly—and immediately—in such situations, disaster may ensue.

But it's not just police officers who need training. Teachers must be trained to deal quickly and efficiently with disruptive classroom situations. Otherwise, the room will be in constant chaos. For medical professionals, administering emergency life-saving measures must become practically second-nature. None of us likes to think of our surgeon standing over our open abdomen and musing, Hamlet-like, "Hmmm. To sew, or not to sew?"

My point is that training is not a bad thing. It's a good thing. All of us, as professionals, require a certain amount of training. But education is something different. Whereas training conditions people to respond without having to think, education prepares them to think. Clearly, both are necessary to equip people for their professions. Unfortunately, what passes for a college education these days is heavily tilted toward the former, with only about three semesters of traditional or classical education (what we sometimes call the "core curriculum") versus five semesters of, essentially, vocational training (the "major" and "minor"). I'm not saying business or engineering or nursing courses don't require critical thinking at all. No doubt, they do. I'm just saying that those courses, of necessity, lean toward training. Most of the specific exposure to critical thinking that students get comes in their English, history, biology, and math classes—all those classes students don't really want to take.

I can relate. I clearly remember sitting in my College Algebra class, as an English major, and wondering, "What the heck am I doing here? Why do I have to take this class? I'll probably never factor another equation as long as I live." And I was right—I haven't factored any equations since. But in another, more important way, I was wrong. What I didn't realize at the time was that learning to think mathematically, disciplining myself to engage my brain and grapple with concepts that didn't come easily to me—which I had to do in order to pass the course—actually expanded my brain capacity. It made me a better thinker.

Because the truth is, we CAN improve our thinking ability. We're not stuck with whatever IQ score was attached to us as children, based on some standardized test. I know this from personal experience, having scored significantly higher on such tests as an adult than I did as a child. (I wonder how much those stupid math classes had to do with that.)

Cross-training for the brain. We CAN expand our brain capacity, but there's only one way to do it, just like there's only one way to expand our physical capacity. We build "mental muscle" in exactly the same way we build our actual muscles: by pushing against resistance, which is how athletes get stronger and body builders get bigger.

That is, or should be, the purpose of a college education—to help us build our mental muscle by providing resistance for us to push against. Moreover, to expand on that metaphor, our brain power grows best when we "cross-train," or push against different types of resistance in different ways—like when nonmath people (like me!) are forced to think mathematically. Or when engineers or scientists are forced to analyze poetry. Most people don't particularly enjoy that kind of thing—remember what I said about thinking not coming naturally to us?—but it is absolutely vital if we are to develop our thinking ability. And, ironically perhaps, it tends to happen most in the courses we like least, the ones that challenge us most and sometimes even make our brains hurt, like sore muscles. That's why I refer sometimes to the core curriculum—those first three semesters of college, when you're taking all those courses you hate—as "cross-training for the brain."

I would invite you, then, to take advantage of the opportunities that come your way, in college and beyond, to expand your intellectual horizons—to learn to think in new and different ways, including ways that are unfamiliar and perhaps uncomfortable. As you do, you will become well-practiced in the first aspect of critical thinking: actually thinking.

Critical Thinking Is Critical

The second characteristic of critical thinking is that it is "critical." But what does that mean, in this context? This is where I believe a great deal of the misunderstanding lies—the source of the disconnect between what employers want (and say they're not getting) and what colleges claim to be teaching.

In our modern parlance, the word "critical" almost always means something negative. To "criticize" is to find fault or point out weaknesses. But that's not really what it means, in the context of "critical thinking"—or at least not what it's supposed to mean in the classical sense of the term. For our purposes, the closest synonym for "critical" is not "negative" but rather "neutral." To think critically means to approach a concept from a neutral or objective position, not simply to attack it as if it's automatically bad.

Think, for example, of someone who writes movie reviews for a living. We refer to that person as a "movie critic," by which we do not mean that they constantly trash every movie they see. Rather, we expect them to give us an unbiased and professional assessment of the film, based on their knowledge of how films work (or fail to work) and many years of experience. No doubt they've seen thousands of films. And so we trust them to (a) know whether a movie is any good, and (b) tell us what they think and why. (Note that we still might not accept what they say at face value; we might still want to see the movie for ourselves. But when we read reviews, we do so to at least get an idea of what to expect.) In other words, we trust the critic to be objective, analytical, and dispassionate, taking into account all of the relevant factors.

Critical equals "objective." Of course, the movie critic is ultimately expressing an opinion, telling us what they think about the movie. We get that. We understand that it's just one person's opinion. At the same time, we assume they probably know more about movies than we do, having seen so many of them and written about them for reputable publications, perhaps for many years. If they weren't any good at being a movie critic, they probably wouldn't still be doing it for a living.

More important, we assume that they are being objective, evaluating the movie based on its merits (or lack of same) and not on how they happen to feel about it personally or on other, external factors. Obviously, it's impossible for anyone to be completely objective. We're all human, each with our own set of biases, some of which we're aware of and some of which, quite frankly, we're not. That's part of the human condition. (Although learning to recognize and account for those biases is an important component of critical thinking, as we will see later.) So we don't expect the movie critic to be perfect or superhuman—but we do have a reasonable expectation that they have made every attempt to take a step back from those biases, whatever they may be, and analyze the movie as objectively as possible.

That means, among other things, that they have taken a neutral position going in, rather than pre-judging the movie (note that "pre-judging" is what "prejudice" means) based on such things as their own personal likes and dislikes, their political views, or their mood at the time. Let's say that a particular critic doesn't really care for comic book movies, for instance, but they're assigned by their publication to review the latest Marvel offering. As readers, we should be able to assume that their personal preferences will not cloud their judgment—that they won't decide, beforehand, that the movie can't possibly be any good because it's in a genre they dislike. In order to analyze it effectively, they have to be more objective than that.

Critical equals "analytical." Which brings me to my next point: that the word "critical" refers to the cognitive process of analysis. To understand what that means in this context, think of the word "analyze" as it is used in science—for instance, in chemistry. Perhaps you have analyzed compounds in a high school or college chemistry course. What does that mean? It means that you literally break the chemical down into its component parts, in order to see what it's composed of and thereby gain a better understanding of its nature. That is an element of critical thinking.

Again, think of our movie critic. How are they going to approach their review? How are they going to tell us what's good, bad, or indifferent about the movie and why? Quite possibly by breaking the film down and looking at its various parts. Perhaps the cinematography is breathtaking but the costumes are cheesy. Maybe the actors do yeoman's work in rescuing a terrible script—or vice-versa. Or maybe the entire film could have benefited from having a director more attuned to detail. Ultimately, what makes the movie work or not are all of those items, separately and working together. As readers, we can't really understand where the reviewer is coming from, why they reached the conclusions they did, without having it broken down for us. That's analysis.

Critical equals "dispassionate." Perhaps the most important aspect of critical thinking is that it's dispassionate. Obviously, the word "passion" has to do with emotions, so "dispassionate" means something like "without emotion." Except, in this case, that's not exactly what it means. No one is suggesting that we have to completely ignore our emotions or become unfeeling drones. Rather, to be dispassionate means that we're able, first of all, to recognize emotions for what they are and then give them the proper weight in our thinking processes, which may range from a lot to none at all.

Let's face it, as human beings we are highly emotional creatures. We make LOTS of decisions based on emotion. And I'm not saying that's always a bad thing. Perhaps there are some decisions that should be made that way, such as affairs of the heart, for instance. (Although, even there, I'd recommend giving your head a vote. Just a suggestion.) But there are clearly some decisions, in life and especially as professionals, that we cannot base solely or even primarily on emotional factors.

For example, let's say you're a manager of a small department with twelve employees. Word comes down from your superiors that, due to budget cuts, you have to lay two people off. How do you make that decision? Can you base it solely, or even primarily, on which people in the office you like or dislike the most? Is that fair? Or must you weigh other factors as well, such as salaries and productivity? Or should you consider those kinds of factors—the "data"—exclusively and not take emotion into account at all?

The answer, I think, is that it depends. There's no one-size-fits-all approach when it comes to tough decisions like these. But I would say that, in general, in order to think critically in this situation, you first have to recognize the emotional factors for what they are and set them aside, at least for the moment. Then look at all the other relevant factors. At some point, all things being equal, your decision may come down to emotional factors. Perhaps two individuals in your office have the same salary and are similarly productive, but you have a personality conflict with one of them. That's a legitimate concern, in cases like this, even if it is based largely on emotion.

The bottom line is that, even if your final decision is ultimately based partly on emotion, it is not based solely on emotion. More importantly, you are not acting in ignorance, being led by emotion without even realizing it. Quite frankly, that is what most people do most of the time, and it's a difficult habit to break. Learning not to be controlled by our emotions requires no small amount of discipline on our part. That discipline is developed in part through our educational experiences as we cross-train our brain, learning to evaluate emotionally charged subject matter—like a literary work or a historical event—without allowing our emotions to overcome our reason.

Let's go back to our movie critic one more time. Suppose they had family members who died during the Holocaust, and they're reviewing a film that depicts that time period—like, say, *Schindler's List* or *Sophie's Choice*. Should we expect them to put that completely out of their mind, to ignore their own emotional response to the subject matter? No. That's not a reasonable expectation. What we can reasonably expect, though, is that they're able to say whether the film is any good or not—and to make a compelling case for their viewpoint, either way—based largely on their professional judgment and not just on how it made them feel.

Or consider another example. Let's say that ten years ago, our movie critic was supposed to interview a famous actor, but he blew her off. Now, ten years later, our critic is still trashing every movie that actor makes, even the ones that have gotten good reviews from other critics. Would we consider that to be acceptable behavior? Of course not. We expect critics to behave more professionally than that. We expect them to be able to set aside their (perhaps understandable) anger and disappointment and evaluate that actor's movies objectively. That's what it means to be dispassionate.

Critical equals "questioning." Finally, although being critical doesn't necessarily mean being negative, it does involve questioning—questioning the things people say, the things we read, the things we see on television or on the Internet, the ways things have always been done. That doesn't mean those things are always wrong; it just means that, as an educated person and an independent thinker, you shouldn't just assume they're automatically right. You must always maintain a healthy skepticism.

Note, however, that there's a difference between skepticism and cynicism. The latter is indeed a negative viewpoint, one that always assumes the worst. Cynics don't just decline to believe everything they're told; they often refuse to believe ANYTHING they're told. They assume that everyone is either lying or just plain stupid and that pretty much everybody (but them) has ulterior motives. That attitude may well have been acquired honestly at the school of hard knocks, but allow me to suggest that it is no way to live. Besides being depressing, it makes no more sense to insist that everything is always wrong than it does to argue that everything is always right. Nor is cynicism a form of critical thinking; rather, it is the negation of critical thinking, implying that using our brain is pointless because it won't help matters, anyway. In essence, cynicism is a form of defeatism.

Skepticism, on the other hand, always holds open the possibility that what we're reading or hearing or seeing may in fact be correct. It just stops short of assuming that those things are always correct. Instead of automatically denying or rejecting, the skeptic seeks to discover whether an idea is right or wrong, through questioning, research, and earnest contemplation. It is this sort of healthy skepticism that often prevents us from taking wrong paths merely because they seem attractive or popular. Rather than blindly accepting whatever information is presented to us, we look at each piece objectively, break it down analytically, and evaluate it dispassionately.

Remember what I said about educated people not being easily led? That's because they're always questioning—much to the dismay of politicians and advertisers, who want us just to accept whatever they say at face value and vote for them or buy their products, no questions asked.

Critical thinking or "critique"? So why the disconnect? Given the above definition of critical thinking, which I believe is the true definition, why do employers still complain that college graduates can't do it, even as colleges and universities are shouting from the rooftops that they're teaching it—and, in many cases, congratulating themselves effusively for teaching it so well?

The answer is that, very often, what colleges are teaching under the banner of "critical thinking" isn't really critical thinking, at least not as I've defined it. Nor, evidently, are they teaching what employers want their graduates to learn. Instead, many college courses teach a version of critical thinking that focuses on the negative definition of the word "critical"—the word they use is "critique," which we'll define in a moment—and actually eschews thinking in favor of feeling.

I often tell my students, when they begin a comment with the words "I feel," that I'm not really concerned about how they feel. Of course I care about them as human beings, and I'll be happy to talk with them after class, if they think that will help. If they have serious issues that I'm not equipped to deal with, I'll be glad to refer them to one of our professional counselors on campus. But during class, in the context of our discussions, I'm much more concerned with what they THINK than with what they FEEL. There's a difference. Thinking and feeling are not the same thing. And many of our society's problems, I'm convinced, stem from our collective inability to distinguish between the two. As we've already seen, solutions to problems based primarily on emotions aren't always effective, nor are they necessarily fair to everyone concerned. That's because our emotions, our feelings, are changeable, unpredictable, and entirely subjective. To make good decisions, we need information that is more stable and reliable, which is where objective, dispassionate analysis comes in.

Unfortunately, much of what's taught on today's college campuses, especially in humanities and social science courses, isn't about thinking—it's about feeling. This trend can be traced back at least to the mid-1980s, with the emergence of a literary theory known as "deconstruction." (And probably farther than that, but that's as far back as I need to go for our purposes here. If you're really interested in learning more about this topic, look up "The Frankfort School.") Advanced most notably by the French philosopher and literary critic Jacques Derrida, deconstruction basically posits that literary texts cannot ultimately be deciphered with any real confidence because the meaning of the language is constantly shifting. We tend to believe that words have specific meanings and that we can therefore interpret them. Not necessarily, said Derrida. For him, meaning was relative, dependent on historical and social context and ultimately on the experiences of the reader.

In other words, we have for decades studied literary works and tried to figure out what they mean. That, according to Derrida, is pointless. You can never determine what a work means—you can only determine what it means to *you*. Thus meaning itself becomes entirely subjective. As a literary theory, this is mildly interesting and perhaps even a bit thought-provoking. Perhaps it is true that meaning in literary works is highly subjective, since no two critics seem to agree on what a poem or story means, anyway. (Which is still a far cry from saying it doesn't mean anything at all. But let's leave that aside for a moment.)

The problem is that this theory began to creep into other academic areas, not only in the humanities but in the social sciences. For the latter, that is particularly problematic because any discipline with the word "science" in its name ought to be focused on finding the truth. But what if there is no ultimate truth to be found? What if all meaning really is relative, not just in literary texts, but in history, sociology, political science—even science itself? What if "truth" is not an objective reality but merely a subjective construct, utterly dependent on our perceptions or how we happen to "feel" about whatever we're studying?

Obviously, such beliefs run contrary to the long-understood mission of higher education, which is to get at the truth (or as close as we can, anyway). And that is precisely the issue. In many college courses these days, students are not being taught to pursue truth as something tangible and definable. Instead, they are taught to "deconstruct," which means to criticize or "critique" existing social structures. Everything is bad and must be attacked and torn down, whether it's objectively bad or not.

Because, remember, deconstruction isn't about being objective. Rather, it privileges subjectivity. It's all about how you feel. If you don't like something you see, perhaps because you perceive it as unjust—aka, "not fair"—then it must necessarily be bad, whether or not you've actually taken time to think it through and consider all the evidence. And so it needs to be destroyed or replaced, even if you're actually "fixing" a nonexistent problem or if your "fixes" ultimately make things worse.

At the risk of repeating myself, that's not critical thinking. It's "critique," which sounds like it might be the same thing but is actually, as a colleague of mine recently put it, "the ruthless criticism of all that exists." And therein lies the disconnect. Employers don't want people just to ruthlessly criticize their "existing systems." They don't want to hire people just to "deconstruct." They're looking for people who can think critically, which may entail a certain amount of critique, in the sense of asking hard questions, as we discussed above. But mostly it's about approaching problems objectively and dispassionately and reasoning through them using logic and reason based on evidence—and then communicating solutions clearly in writing.

That, once again, is the dual purpose of this book: to correct any misconceptions readers might have about critical thinking while showing them how to actually think critically and then help them hone their writing skills. Those two abilities—thinking and writing—are virtually inseparable, as we shall see in the chapters that follow.

HOW TO THINK CRITICALLY

You might think the title of this chapter sounds a little ambitious, and you would be right. Entire books have been written on this topic alone. So you're probably thinking there's no way I can cover it thoroughly in one short chapter of what is, after all, a fairly short book. And again, you would be right.

Fortunately, that's not my objective. I realize there's no way I can talk about every conceivable aspect of critical thinking in one chapter, and maybe not even in this entire book—but I'm not trying to. My purpose in writing in this book, as I've said, is to identify some of the fundamentals of critical thinking and clear writing, for people who might not have been exposed to these ideas before (or who may have been exposed to them but promptly forgot), in a way that's easy to read and understand and that will help them improve their skills. In this particular chapter, my objective is to summarize and reiterate some of the key points I've already made while introducing important new points I'll be exploring in subsequent chapters.

In other words, this chapter is intended more as an outline than a full-fledged discussion. At the same time, I hope it serves as a handy "pocket guide" to some of these principles—a chapter that readers can return to anytime they need a quick refresher, or if they wish to share the principles with others in a succinct and accessible way. We'll continue to touch on many of these concepts in the chapters that follow, as a way of reiterating and expanding on the main points.

With that in mind, and acknowledging that everyone from professors to employers is constantly demanding that you need to be a better critical thinker—well, how do you go about that? How exactly does one think critically?

Start with Curiosity

One of the main reasons people fail to think critically is that they don't even try. We could call this intellectual laziness, and perhaps in some cases it is, but for the most part that's probably a bit harsh. The truth is, people are busy. They're constantly looking for the path of least resistance, not necessarily because they're lazy—although, as I said, that can be the case—but because they have a lot on their plate and are simply trying to get one thing off as fast as possible before moving on to the next.

Alternatively, they may not see something as particularly important, worth spending much time thinking about. In that calculation, they are all too often mistaken. People are constantly screwing up—myself included—because we don't pay enough attention to something that we thought was trivial or minor but turned out to be important. And that's true, by the way, in our personal as well as professional lives.

As I mentioned back in Chapter 2, people also aren't used to thinking critically— or even having to really think at all. Thinking is hard work. We've constructed this entire technologically advanced society around our desire not to have to think about stuff too much. And so we don't, even when we should. (But consider this: You know the people who created all that technology so the rest of us don't have to think too much? They obviously had to put a lot of thought into it. Is it any wonder they're the ones getting filthy rich?)

So the first step to thinking critically is simply wanting to—acknowledging that something requires a bit of thought and then putting the necessary time and energy into actually thinking it through. I mentioned in Chapter 2 that critical thinking is, in large part, about asking questions. Let me expand on that a bit here by saying that it begins with the *willingness* to ask questions, followed by the recognition that questions need to be asked, and then the actual questions themselves. That willingness to ask questions, along with the perseverance to follow through, is a mindset—one that I believe we can train ourselves to adopt. If we want to put a label on that mindset, we might call it *intellectual curiosity*.

We usually think of intellectual curiosity in terms of academic subjects. But note that the word "intellectual" here merely has to do with using our brains. We can be intellectually curious about anything, from the motives of our politicians to the basis for our company's new policy; from the effects of a natural disaster on the stock market to the reasons our checking account is overdrawn.

To put it another way, one of the reasons people don't think critically in some cases is because they don't bother to ask questions. Perhaps they're afraid of the answer, or afraid of what might happen to them if they rock the boat. Perhaps they really are lazy and just don't bother asking questions, even if they know they should. Or perhaps—worst of all—they simply take everything they hear or read at face value and assume that no curiosity is required. That is precisely what the people who are trying to control our behavior, from politicians to advertisers to overbearing bosses, are hoping for.

They say "curiosity killed the cat," but I would argue that lack of curiosity has probably killed a lot more than just a few cats (not that cats aren't awesome), including many a career, more than a few business ventures, and maybe even a civilization or two. Asking questions can be uncomfortable, for ourselves and those around us. It can be kind of scary, as we put our reputations and careers on the line. The risks are real; other people—those who are trying to control us—often don't like us to ask questions.

We just have to ask questions, anyway. You may be familiar with the story of "The Emperor's New Clothes," about two con men, claiming to be weavers, who promise a particularly vain emperor that they can make him the most beautiful suit of clothes ever. The catch is that only the best and wisest people in the kingdom will be able to see it. When the emperor looks in on them, he sees the two charlatans madly at work on their loom—but he can see no actual cloth. Of course, he doesn't say anything, because that would mean he is neither good nor wise. It isn't until the silly monarch parades through the streets in his flashy new "outfit," with the townspeople all exclaiming how marvelous he looks, that one little boy tugs on his mother's skirt and blows up the entire fraudulent scheme by asking a pointed question: "Momma, why is the Emperor naked?"

And by the way, when I talk about "the people who are trying to control us," I'm not advancing some dark conspiracy theory. It's simply a fact that people in a position to do so are constantly trying to exert control over others' behavior—to get them to do what they want them to do. That includes the politicians, advertisers, and bosses I mentioned above, but it also includes teachers, religious leaders, and the media. They all want us to do or think certain things, most of which are harmless and some of which might even be beneficial. But some of the things they want us to do—like buy a product we can't afford or accept a policy that's immoral—actually run contrary to our best interests. Later, when we talk about argument and persuasion, we'll see how this works and how you can actually use specific techniques and strategies to get people to do what *you* want. In the meantime, though, learning to think critically is the only way to prevent others from exerting an undue and perhaps detrimental influence over you.

Of course, not all questions are "critical" in the negative sense. Many are merely, well, curious. Consider how our understanding of gravity was enlightened by Sir Isaac Newton, who (according to legend) began by simply wondering why an apple fell from a tree. The point is that, to be effective critical thinkers, we must develop the intellectual habit of questioning everything, whether it seems important or trivial, innocuous or sinister.

Be Honest with Yourself

As long as we're in a questioning mode, one of our main subjects ought to be ourselves. Even if we're making a genuine attempt to think critically about some issue, our own subconscious beliefs can sometimes be an obstacle without our even realizing it. We can reach wrong conclusions because we begin with the wrong assumptions. Most of the time, though, as I suggested above, we're not even really trying to think critically. In those cases, we tend just to go with our assumptions without even questioning them—and that can create major problems when those assumptions turn out to be wrong.

Questioning assumptions. You've probably heard the old saying that to "assume" makes an "ass" out of "u" and "me." That can certainly be true, as I've learned the hard way on more than one occasion. Several years ago, for instance, my oldest daughter applied for an academic scholarship at the college where she had been accepted. She had taken several college courses as a dual enrollment student while still in high school and done quite well. The scholarship committee factored those grades into their decision and she was awarded a scholarship. Two years later, when her brother applied to the same institution, we assumed they would look at his dual enrollment grades, too, and that he would likewise receive a scholarship. We didn't realize the policy had changed—mostly because we didn't question our assumption or bother to look up the information. That mistake cost our family several thousand dollars.

I'm not saying assumptions are always bad. In reality, assumptions are nothing more than subconscious hypotheses (which we're going to talk about more in the next section). Like all hypotheses, they can be either correct or incorrect. I look out the window on a fine spring morning, see that the sun is shining, flowers are blooming, and birds are flitting from tree to tree, and I assume that I probably won't need a heavy coat for my afternoon walk. As I open the front door, I discover that I was correct. It is indeed a nice day, and I don't need my coat. Or perhaps I learn that I was wrong; despite the sunshine, there's a cool breeze, and I do need a jacket. Either way, I benefit.

Thus, the value in learning to question our assumptions is twofold. If, upon further examination, we learn that we were wrong, we have the opportunity to change our hypothesis. That can sometimes be painful, but it's probably better than just going around be wrong all the time. On the other hand, if our examination provides evidence that we were correct all along, then our hypothesis becomes an actual argument—an assertion supported by evidence.

Recognizing biases. Some assumptions, however, are more deeply held and relatively permanent. We call these biases. We tend to think of "bias" as an ugly word, but once again, not all biases are necessarily bad. Some are quite harmless. For example, I was born in the Southern United States and have lived in the South all my life. I love it here. I have absolutely no interest in living in the Northeast. Why not? It's hard to say. I don't know if I can adequately put it into words. It's simply a deeply held preference—in other words, a bias in favor of the South.

Note that, for the most part, this particular bias is pretty harmless. I'm an adult, and this is a free country. I can live where I want. I don't dislike people from the Northeast, much less discriminate against them in any way. I just don't want to live there myself (although I love to visit). What's wrong with that?

Well, nothing . . . unless . . . what if I were offered a really good job, doing something I've always wanted to do, making lots of money, but the job just happened to be located in, say, Boston, Massachusetts. Would it be rational to turn it down just because it's in the Northeast? To be clear, there might be plenty of good reasons to turn down the job: I don't want to be that far from my aging parents; the cost of living in Boston is much higher than where I live now, so that even with a salary increase, my family and I would have a lower quality of life; I don't want to take my kids out of their current school. The list could go on.

But that's exactly the point. Recognizing and taking all those factors into account—a process that would begin, by the way, with questions like "Can we afford to live there?" and "How would it affect the kids?"—involves critical think- ing. That's what critical thinking is, and it's precisely what I'm supposed to do in that situation. Turning down the job just because it's in Boston, however, is NOT thinking critically. It's just a knee-jerk response based on a bias, a feeling that I might not fully understand or even be aware of.

So any bias CAN BE harmful, including one that seems relatively innocent. And of course some forms of bias are more inherently harmful than others—like racism, sexism, and so forth. We all know those feelings are wrong, but the prob- lem is, we might not be fully aware that we harbor them. We all probably think, for example, that we're not the least bit racist or sexist, but if we really examine our behavior, we might be mortified to learn that we do, in fact, sometimes make decisions or judge people based on race or sex. We might find that we do, in fact, hold views that, upon closer examination, turn out to be unjust.

Don't get me wrong—I'm not saying everybody is racist or sexist. I'm just saying that, over our lifetimes, we all develop powerful underlying assumptions about people and situations that we might not even be aware of. We've got to be willing to look objectively at what's going on around us, acknowledge reality, and ask serious questions—even regarding our own actions. If you're a white male supervisor, and you observe that the women and minorities in your department generally don't make as much money or get promoted as often as the white men, you might want to ask yourself why that is. There may be perfectly logical, legit- imate reasons, having to do with things like seniority and productivity, in which case you should be able to offer a persuasive defense should anyone question the apparent disparities.

Then again, if you're being honest with yourself, you might NOT be able to identify any legitimate reasons, in which case you can begin taking steps to rectify the situation. Either way, if you want to continue to grow and evolve as a human being—not to mention do a good job and not open yourself up to lawsuits—it's vital that you pay attention to what's going on, ask the right questions, and recog- nize that your own subconscious biases just might be at work.

Fortunately, most biases aren't as ugly or dramatic as racism or sexism. Yet even apparently simple, supposedly harmless biases—like not wanting to live in a particular region or preferring one brand name to another just because we think it's "cool"—can still keep us from making the right decisions. The key is to recog- nize biases for what they are. Then we can deal with them accordingly.

Do Your Homework

Once you've started asking the right questions, while being honest with yourself about your own assumptions and biases, you may well discover that you don't have all the answers to those questions. That's where research comes in.

I know that for a lot of people, especially college students, *research* can be an ugly word, conjuring up images of long, boring papers, hours spent in the library, and sleepless all-nighters. And sometimes, that is indeed what research requires.

Keep in mind, though, that in the real world, the world beyond college, research is not simply an empty intellectual exercise. Rather, the purpose of research is to answer questions. We do this all the time, often without even being aware of it. We scan through the want-ads looking for a part-time job or an apartment. We Google "how many times has Tom Brady been MVP" to win an argument with a buddy. We pull out our phone and say, "Hey, Siri, Chili's restaurant near me." Those are all example of research—seeking answers to our legitimate questions.

In professional life, as in college, often the questions are given to us, from "why were sales down by six percent last month" to "what was the impact of trade on French colonialism." In both cases, the only way to find the answer is to consult sources, whether those happen to be journals in the library or a company spreadsheet. The principle is the same. It's all research—what we sometimes call "doing our homework." (And for college students, it literally is homework.)

As an aspect of critical thinking, though, research is usually about finding answers to our OWN questions, the ones we pose for ourselves. Those may well be connected to the questions that other people (like our bosses) pose for us; if we're really on the ball, we might even have anticipated their questions and started pursuing answers on our own. That's what's known in the professional world as being a "self-starter," and it is a highly valued trait. In fact, when managers complain that employees can't "think for themselves," that is a largely what they mean. They want people with the ability to recognize potential issues and problems, ask the right questions, and then set out to find answers all on their own, without having to be told exactly what to do every step of the way.

In other words, they want employees who can think critically—and a big part of that, beyond asking the right questions, is finding the right answers.

And by the way, this isn't just a job skill. It's a life skill, as valuable in our personal lives as in our professional lives. Not sure if what you heard on the news or what some politician said is correct? Do some research. Want to know how much sunlight those azaleas need before you decide where to plant them? Look it up. Wondering whether your car insurance covers a rental? Read your policy. Again, these are all forms of practical research that enable us to make considered, thoughtful, rational decisions based on evidence, rather than being controlled by our emotions, going along with the crowd, or doing something stupid because we didn't know better—even though we should have.

Finding and evaluating sources. Doing your research is great, but frankly it probably won't help much if your sources are faulty or suspect. That means you can't just go to any old source—like the first site that happens to pop up on the Internet. You have to evaluate your sources, which in itself requires a certain amount of critical thinking. In particular, this is where questioning and especially a healthy skepticism come in. Frankly, you shouldn't take anything at face value, unless it's a source you have good reason to trust (like your partner or a family doctor, for instance).

Evaluating sources can be challenging, because there are so many of them and they are often in conflict. How do we know who or what is correct? In some cases, there is no way to be absolutely certain, but there are some guidelines for getting the best possible information and thus making the best possible decisions.

First, when it comes to published sources, a good rule of thumb is that the more people involved in the decision to publish, the more likely a source is to be reliable. In this scenario, academic journals are at the top of the pecking order, because they not only rely on multiple editors and reviewers, but many of those people are reading blind—that is, they don't even know who the author is, so they're less likely to be biased. This is known as "peer review." Books, magazines, and newspapers all have editors, as well, if not as many (or as unbiased). And at the bottom of the heap would be "Joe's Blog," because they only person involved in the decision to publish there is Joe.

Of course, evaluating sources based on this principle is an inexact science. If Joe happens to be a renowned test pilot, and he's writing about aviation, then his blog is a reliable, authoritative source—because he is an authority. But if he's writing about gardening, maybe not so much. Conversely, just because several people were involved in the decision to publish a book or article, that doesn't automatically make it credible. It's just somewhat more likely to be credible than, say a book on the same topic that was self-published. You still have to evaluate each source carefully and decide for yourself how much faith you're willing to put in one versus another.

Common sense, practical knowledge, and the "reasonable person" test. Another key to evaluating various (and sometimes conflicting) sources is to apply the "reasonable person" test. This is sometimes referred to as "using common sense," but in my experience, it isn't all that common. The reasonable person test involves applying your own powers of observation, knowledge of the world, and understanding of human nature. You know that old saying, "If it sounds too good to be true, it probably is"? That's because we understand intuitively that no one is going to give you a free vacation to Florida and expect absolutely nothing in return. The world just doesn't work that way, and we all know it. So our immediate response, if we have half a brain, is to ask, "Okay, what's the catch?"

Likewise, if I read an article that begins with the premise that most people are motivated by love and kindness, I might tend to give it less credence, since

I've observed (not to sound too cynical) that most people seem to be motivated by self-interest. Or if some politician asserts that an AR-15 model semi-automatic rifle can fire "150 rounds in 15 seconds," because I happen know a little about guns, I'm going to say, "Um, I don't think so." That's applying common sense and practical knowledge to my evaluation of information—in other words, using the reasonable person test.

We do have to be a little careful, however, because there are things that seem completely counter-intuitive, like there's no way they could be true, yet they turn out to be true, anyway—such as the fact that there are ten times as many bacteria cells than human cells in the typical human body. And yes, that is true. We have to be open-minded when we encounter information that seems dubious, but we also have to be a bit skeptical. If the information doesn't seem to pass the reasonable person test, keep researching. You may find out it's true, after all—or you may find out you were right, and it is "fake news."

More is better. Which brings me to my last point: The best way to get to "the truth" (or as close as we can come, anyway) is to consult a number of different sources, including those that disagree with each other. In other words, gather as much information as you can, from a variety of perspectives. Consider each source and decide how credible it's likely to be. Think about what each source says, comparing it to other sources and applying the reasonable person test. Then, after all that effort, and all that thinking (there's that word again), reach the best, most logical conclusion you can, and based on that, decide what you think is true and how you should respond.

If you follow that pattern consistently, you will still occasionally be wrong, because sometimes even the best information is faulty, and—let's face it—no one is right all the time. But you will not be wrong very often. For the most part, you will get it right—because you went to the trouble of thinking critically about an issue and not just dismissing it or acting on a whim. And even if you are wrong occasionally, there's a way to correct for that. It's called the Scientific Method.

Apply the Scientific Method

Remember those Milesians, from Chapter 2? They invented a form of philosophical debate they called "critical reasoning," which is the basis for today's critical thinking (in the classical sense of that term, not the postmodern sense). For the Milesians, critical reasoning involved formulating, proposing, and examining hypotheses—very much like today's "scientific method." In fact, it's so similar to the scientific method that I think we can conclude that the scientific method isn't just about "science," as we normally use the term. It's really just a guide for thinking critically and thus can be applied to the pursuit of knowledge in general. (Remember that the Latin root for our word "science" merely means "to know.")

Specifically, the scientific method provides a structure for helping us examine our own thinking to see if we're on the right track. As you may remember from your high-school science classes, the scientific method consists of three steps: observing, forming hypotheses, and testing those hypotheses. Of course, we're observing all the time, whether we realize it or not (which is not the same as saying we're always particularly observant). And, as we've already established, we are constantly forming hypotheses, at least of the unconscious variety. We call those "assumptions." The salient questions are, first, to what extent do we acknowledge or even recognize our assumptions? And second, how thoroughly do we follow through and examine them? That second activity is what we call "testing."

Observation. As I noted above, we're always observing, even if we're not always paying much attention to what we observe. As part of the scientific method, however, observation becomes a much more conscious and intentional activity. It involves actively paying attention to the situation, attempting purposefully to figure out what's going on.

We can certainly apply that strategy to people's behavior. Successful individuals are often keen observers of human nature. They pay close attention to what's happening around them—the way people act, the things they say, the patterns that emerge, the underlying causes, and the resulting effects. They file those observations away and use them later to interpret new, emerging situations—or even to predict events that haven't taken place yet. Many times, this seems to put them ahead of the curve. A simple example would be someone who plays the stock market and notices that, every time the Federal Reserve even mentions raising interest rates, stock prices tend to fall. An astute investor can parlay that observation into profit, by buying or selling stocks accordingly.

We also use this skill when we read or listen to what people have say—although in this case, we need to add another word before "read" and "listen." That word is "closely," meaning we paying close and careful attention to what we're reading or hearing. The folks in the white lab coats, the scientists, don't just check in on the rats occasionally to see what they're up to; they watch them carefully for hours on end, taking careful notes. Clearly, "observing" means something more than just watching, reading, or listening. It requires much greater focus, concentration, and effort.

And by the way, speaking of the folks in lab coats, what exactly are they looking for? The answer is, they're looking for *anomalies*. An anomaly is something odd, out of character, or unexpected. If all the rats are just running around behaving like, well, rats, that's not particularly helpful or informative. But when one of the rats does something strange or unusual, like spinning in circles, for instance, the scientists suddenly take notice. What just happened? Why? What caused it? What might it lead to? All those questions stem from close observation—and lead naturally to the next step: forming hypotheses.

Hypothesizing. If an assumption is a subconscious hypothesis, then what we're talking about here is actively forming *conscious* hypotheses, based on careful observation—that is, on doing your homework. In other words, you study the problem as closely and carefully as possible, decide what you believe to be true based on your observations, and then use that information to form a hypothesis.

For example, let's say you're a buyer for the women's department at a large retailer. One February, you notice that swimsuits are selling unusually well for the time of year—in fact, you're sold out. That's never happened before, in your experience. Usually, swimsuit sales don't pick up until March or April. The obvious question is, why the sudden upswing in February swimsuit sales? Is it an anomaly? A trend? Should you order a new shipment? More to the point, should you be sure to order more swimsuits the following December, to be prepared for the February rush? What if you order a bunch of swimsuits and they don't sell? You could be forced to discount them early, costing the store a bunch of money.

So what would you do? Obviously, you'd try to find the answers to those questions. You'd probably talk to your counterparts at other stores, question your sales staff to see if they have any insights, maybe even ask—or have the salespeople ask—the customers, using nonintrusive questions like, "I love this swimsuit. Are you headed to the beach?" In other words, you would do your homework. You would study the question as thoroughly as possible, from as many different angles as possible. That's observation.

Maybe, in the process of researching and asking questions, you discover that the local school system has just moved up the dates of its annual spring break from April to March. You hypothesize, then, that this development explains the sudden surge in February swimsuit sales—women and girls are indeed headed to the beach. From that, you conclude that it would definitely be a good idea to have more swimsuits in stock next February, and that as long as the schools keep those same spring break dates, the suits will probably sell just fine. That is a rational hypothesis, a reasonable conclusion derived from your careful, diligent observation of the situation.

In this kind of scenario, which is pretty common in professional life, there's really just one viable hypothesis. However, some situations present more than one. That is, there might be a number of possible reasons why something is happening. One of the keys to applying the scientific method, then, is the ability to entertain multiple possibilities at once rather than becoming locked, early on, into a single hypothesis. That requires us to remain open-minded as we examine the situation, and it also goes back to my point about unconscious biases. If we find ourselves becoming married to a single hypothesis, despite the objective fact that other explanations are, at that point, equally viable, that's probably because one of our biases has surfaced—which is why rooting those out and coming to recognize them early in the process is such a key aspect of critical thinking.

Ultimately, however, we must narrow the possibilities down to a single hypothesis—what we think is happening and the implications of that for our decision-making moving forward. But how can we know if that really is the best path? That's where the next step comes in—testing.

Testing. This step really cuts to the heart of the scientific method. Remember what we learned back in Chapter 2 about "falsifiability"—the idea that, in order for a hypothesis to be valid, people must be able to test it and, theoretically at least, show it to be false? That's really just another way of saying that a hypothesis has to be testable. It might be right, or it might be wrong. The only way to know is to try it out.

Testing is also key to critical thinking. It's great if we ask questions, do our homework, think things through, and reach what seems to be a logical conclusion. But how do we know if it's really a logical conclusion? How do we know we're right? The answer is simple: We put it to the test, or if possible a series of tests, and see if it holds up.

This sort of testing is common practice in fields that require people to use critical thinking skills everyday—that is, to think things through thoroughly and carefully or else risk disaster. Picture automotive engineers track-testing a new design. They have to get it right or people could die—and their company could be bankrupted by lawsuits. Same with pharmaceutical testing. Software designers test new computer code over and over to try to identify and eliminate any bugs before it's released to the public. (The fact that they don't always catch all the bugs is beside the point. Imagine if they didn't bother testing it at all!)

The same principles apply to any sort of decision-making, even when it's not a matter of life and death (or solvency versus insolvency). Let's go back to our swimsuit dilemma. After investigating the situation as thoroughly as possible, and thinking it through carefully, you decide to buy three times as many swimsuits the following year, hypothesizing that since spring break will once again be in March, you will probably sell a lot of those suits in February—and won't be left holding the bag, with a bunch of unsold swimsuits on your hands. Ultimately, the only way to know for sure if you're correct is to hang the suits on the display racks in February and see if they actually sell. If so, you're on to something and will probably keep doing the same thing year after year, at least as long as spring break remains in March. If not, then you'll take the hit financially and not buy all those suits the following year. Either way, you won't know if your hypothesis is correct until you test it.

Of course, it isn't always practical or even feasible to "test drive" every decision. In some cases, there may well be common-sense, theoretical "what if" tests you can apply. For example, let's say you're thinking about pursuing a master's degree and looking at graduate schools. In fact, you've narrowed it down to two. How do you make a final decision? Obviously, you should do your homework, starting with logical questions like "How much will it cost?" "Am I eligible for any scholarships?" and "What is the program's job placement rate?" You can easily research all those questions and thereby gather the information you need to make an informed decision about which school to attend or maybe even whether or not to pursue a graduate degree in the first place.

But how do you know if it's the right decision? Well—you don't. No one ever does, really. Most important decisions, to some degree, and some decisions to a great degree, require a leap of faith. But you can gain a little more confidence in your decision, at least, by applying the "what if" test: "What if I graduate with over $100,000 worth of debt? How will that affect my life for the foreseeable future?" "What if the coursework ends up being much harder than I'm anticipating? How will I react?" "What if I'm not able to get the job I want—what then?" If you're satisfied with the answers to those and other questions, then you can move forward with your decision. If not, you might need to give the matter a little more thought.

Note that, in the above scenario, all your research on the different institutions constituted "observation." When you chose one university over the others, that became a hypothesis: "This school is the best choice for me." Those "what if" questions are a way of testing your hypothesis to see if it stands up to scrutiny. Obviously, it's not a perfect system for avoiding mistakes, but it's a whole lot better than what most people seem to do: not thinking things through at all, deciding instead based on a whim or other emotional factors. And since you can't exactly try out one university for a few months before switching to another—well, you can, but it's a major pain and also frowned upon—using the scientific method to consider all the angles probably represents your best chance to make the right call.

As I mentioned at the beginning of this chapter, we're going to be covering a lot of these principles in more detail in the pages that follow. We're also going to see how to apply them in very practical ways. That's the focus of the next chapter.

SOME PRACTICAL APPLICATIONS OF CRITICAL THINKING

Just as it was pretty much impossible, in the last chapter, for me to cover everything under the heading, "How to Think Critically," in this chapter, it's going to be equally difficult to talk about all the many practical applications of critical thinking. Critical thinking, as I hope you're beginning to see, is not just an academic skill; it's a life skill, one that is useful in all sorts of ways and in all kinds of situations. Basically, having both the ability and the presence of mind to think critically in any set of circumstances—at school, at work, in your personal life—is the ultimate practical application of this skill.

However, in this chapter, I want to talk about some of the most important ways that people can use critical thinking in their professional life. (Note that, under the category of "professional," I also include student, if that happens to be your "profession" at the moment.) Some of these "practical applications" might not seem to have much to do with critical thinking, or at least you might not have ever thought of them that way. They might just seem like common sense. Just remember what I said in Chapter 3—that common sense, in my experience, isn't all that common.

To put it another way, these are all areas in which I've observed that many of my college students struggle. I've also discovered, through both formal and informal research—that is, looking at studies and surveys and talking to managers in various industries—that these are the same issues many employees struggle with. And I don't mean to stereotype, but that seems to be especially true of younger employees, the so-called "Millennial Generation." Yes, Gen-X'ers and even Baby Boomers (like me) have their share of challenges when it comes to critical thinking, too. But it seems to me that Millennials have been the chief victims of higher education's decision, about a generation ago, to abandon classical critical thinking in favor of "deconstruction" and Marxist-inspired "critique," as I outlined in Chapter 2. It should be no surprise, then, that Millennials struggle to think critically; as I pointed out, they haven't really been taught to do it. Once again, that's why I wrote this book, and that's who I wrote it for—young people who didn't learn this stuff in college, as well as for my own students, to make sure they're not in the same category one day.

But I digress. My point is that, no, this chapter isn't going to cover every possible way in which you might use critical thinking in your professional (or academic) life. Of course not. But I do plan to talk about some things that I think you will find very useful, things you might not have thought much about before, at least not in the context of critical thinking. My goal is to help you see how critical thinking applies to some of the major tasks and challenges you face everyday, thereby making your life a little easier and enabling you to become a better student, a more competent employee, and, ultimately, a more effective leader.

Time Management

Trying (and generally failing) to establish and maintain a reasonable schedule is one challenge that practically everyone can identify with, from adolescence on up. High-achieving high-school seniors, for instance, must often balance multiple AP courses, and all the homework those entail, with participating in various school activities, applying for colleges, and maybe even holding down a part-time job. Many college students also have jobs, to go along with all their reading, studying, essay-writing, and partying. (Wait. Did I say "partying"? Strike that. I meant to say "participating in study groups.") Somewhere, among all those activities, they also have to find time to do things like eat and sleep. My own experience as a student, as well as my experience raising four teenagers who all became college students, is that the last item on that list—sleep—is usually the first to be sacrificed.

If young people think it's all going to get better once they get out of college and into the "real world," they are, unfortunately, delusional. People starting new careers, "paying their dues," as the saying goes, often spend more hours working than even college students. In fact, they sometimes look back on their college days wistfully, as a relatively stress-free time. Add to that the fact that many people, at that stage in life, get married and start raising children, and you have a potential time-management disaster. Think you didn't get any sleep in college? Just wait until you have a two-month-old.

One reason so many of us struggle with time management is that we don't view it as a problem to be solved—as opposed to a problem merely to be complained about—nor do we see it as an opportunity to put our critical thinking skills to good use. Instead, we just sort of accept an ongoing state of near chaos as simply "the way it is," hoping perhaps that, at some point, it will get better on its own but not taking any positive steps to make things better. Doing so would require self-discipline, to be sure, but it also requires mental discipline. It requires critical thinking.

The first step is to look at the situation objectively—to take a step back, distance ourselves from emotional factors like guilt, personal attachment, and sentimentality, and ask hard questions about our various activities, which might include the following:

- Does this really need to be done?
- Why does it need to be done?

- When does it need to be done?
- Who says so—and what is my relationship to that person?
- Does it need to be done in this way?
- Does it need to be done by me, or can I delegate it?
- If something must be sacrificed in the interests of time, what would cause the least harm?
- What are my goals—that is, what am I actually trying to accomplish?
- Of all the things I'm doing, which ones will help me achieve my goals? Which ones won't?

Those are just a few examples of the questions you might ask if you decided to take a more thoughtful approach to time management, rather than just going about it haphazardly or trusting to luck. Honest answers to these and similar questions should help you trim some of the fat, so to speak, from your schedule while prioritizing the items that remain. Because that is the essence of time management: prioritizing, which requires objectivity, emotional detachment, thoughtful analysis, and honest questioning—all the elements of critical thinking that we talked about in Chapter 3.

Prioritizing also means making value judgments, which may reintroduce an element of subjectivity. (Remember: No one is saying emotions are completely invalid; we just have to recognize them for what they are and weigh them accordingly.) All things being equal, there's nothing wrong with prioritizing activities you enjoy over those you don't enjoy; it's just that all things are rarely equal. Often, the activities you enjoy less (like studying) are more important to your future than those you enjoy more (like partying). Recognizing this truism and acting on it require a certain amount of maturity and clear thinking. But that doesn't mean you can't or shouldn't occasionally attend a party or hit the gym or go camping with friends instead of studying. Mental and physical health should be priorities, too.

In the end, there's no single, one-size-fits-all answer to the problem of time management. That's why doing it well requires critical thinking. Most people don't bother, either because they're too lazy or they just never thought to approach it that way. If you do resolve to take that approach, even if you don't always make the right decision—again, no one does—you will still be light years ahead of those who simply sigh, complain, and settle for chaos.

Problem Solving

In one sense, problem solving is the ultimate application of critical thinking skills, the chief outcome this book is designed to produce. To put it another way, as I pointed out back in Chapter 2, when employers talk about wanting employees who are "critical thinkers," what they really mean, more than anything else, is that they want people who have the ability to think their way through problems and ultimately solve them. "Problem solving" is also a necessarily broad term, because anything that requires thought could be viewed as a problem. Time management, for example, is in essence nothing more than a problem to be solved. I even used that language in talking about it.

All of that said, I am giving problem solving its own section in this chapter because I want to emphasize the fact that it is, in the end, a profoundly practical application of all those elements of critical thinking we talked about in Chapter 3. Problem solving is something you can actually use critical thinking to do. Indeed, it is one of the main things that critical thinking is for. (I also wanted to give time management its own section, since it's such a major challenge for so many of my readers.) If I seem to be repeating myself at times, remember what I said back in Chapter 1: I probably am. And the reasons for that are twofold: (a) All of these concepts are inter-related and overlapping to the extent that it's impossible to talk about them in any depth without occasionally repeating myself; and (b) I don't mind being a little redundant, when it comes to these concepts, because they are the main ideas I want you to take away from your reading and remember for the rest of your life. So if you notice that I seem to be repeating myself, good. That means you're learning.

As a practical application of critical thinking, problem solving consists of two main subapplications, situational analysis and information gathering. Together, they lead naturally to a third main application, which is decision making. But we'll talk about that soon enough.

Situational analysis. For professionals, the decision-making process usually begins with simply figuring out what's going on. That means, first of all, observing what is sometimes referred to as "the situation on the ground"—that is, paying close attention to your surroundings, to what people say and do and the things that happen as a result. We call this "situational analysis." Often, we do it unconsciously, but becoming good critical thinkers requires that we become more intentional about it, as well as "critical" in the sense that we ask the right questions—of ourselves and others.

In fact, questioning is the very next step, right after observation. By this, I mean asking yourself questions like, "What's going on here? How does it differ from what's happened in the past, or from what I might have expected? Whatever is going on, what might have led to it? What might be the result? How does it tie in to any other information I might have?" These are all variations on the traditional "journalism" questions: who, what, when, where, why, and how. (Which is why journalists, in theory at least, are good critical thinkers. Supposedly, they've been trained to be. Unfortunately, that isn't always true these days for people who call themselves journalists.)

Situational analysis may also involve asking questions of others, whether in casual conversation or more formal interviews. Often, to get at the truth—to understand what's really going on—you have to talk to a lot of people and get a variety of different perspectives. Sorting through and balancing those sometimes conflicting accounts may require us to apply the "reasonable person test," in order to figure out what is true or at least what makes the most sense. It may also require us to take our information gathering a step further—but we'll get to that in a moment.

Basically, situational analysis is necessary in order to form a baseline for decision-making. Before you can possibly know what to do in the future, you have to know what's going on in the present. In order to solve a problem, you must understand what the problem is—or at least have a working hypothesis. Analyzing the problem takes us back to the journalism questions: *What* exactly is the problem? For *whom* is it a problem? *Why* is it a problem? *How* big is the problem? These are all questions that must be answered before any reasonable next steps can be considered. And clearly, this requires us to apply critical thinking, rather than just basing our decisions on knee-jerk responses.

Information gathering. But what if the answers to the journalism questions are confusing, or contradictory, or simply difficult to interpret? That's when you have to move beyond observing and questioning and start gathering information from a wider variety of sources. We call this research, and as we learned in Chapter 2, it is a key component of critical thinking. But it's more than that; it's also a way of applying critical thinking skills to practical problem solving. In essence, the more sources you consult, and the more information you can gather, the more likely you are to make the right decision.

Remember our swimsuit dilemma in the last chapter? To figure out what's going on—why swimsuits are suddenly selling so well in February—you might first spend some time pondering the dilemma, trying to think it through, observing "the situation on the ground." Then you would probably talk to a number of people, including sales staff, customers, and colleagues at other stores. Those steps might give you all the information you need—but quite likely not. You will probably also need to look at your company's databases, specifically at sales figures from the current year as compared to past years. Such research—because that's what it is—will give you a firmer sense of whether your observations are correct and whether the things you're hearing have any validity. Together, all that information will enable you to make a rational (and hopefully correct) decision. And note once again that, the more information you have, the more likely it is that your decision will be the right one.

That's a hypothetical scenario, but here is a real one from my days as an academic department chair. In that job, one of my main duties was maintaining a reasonable ratio of full-time and part-time faculty. Plenty of research suggests that having more full-time faculty is better for students. At the same time, as an administrator, it makes sense to have a certain number of part-time faculty, both for budgetary reasons (I never had the money to hire as many full-time people as I wanted) and to provide flexibility in case of enrollment fluctuations. When enrollment shot up, it was a lot quicker, and involved a lot less red tape, to hire part-time faculty to cover those classes. And when enrollment dipped, it was much easier simply not to hire part-timers than to lay off full-timers.

In any case, it was a delicate balancing act, year after year. And each year, when it was time to put in my requests for new full-time faculty, I had to decide what I needed and where. (When I say "where," I'm referring to the fact that my department had several subdepartments. So did I need an English professor more than a speech teacher, or vice-versa?) To make those decisions, I began by thinking about the situation. What was happening in my department? At my institution? Were we growing? Shrinking? At what rate? I also talked to lots of people, including both full- and part-time faculty members, students, and other department chairs, to get their perspective. I read a lot of professional articles about things like budgeting, relevant trends in higher education, and the pros and cons of using part-time faculty. And then I went to the college's databases, where I could find up-to-date, accurate enrollment numbers, completion rates (for students, I mean), and full-time to part-time ratios.

I'm not going to say that I always made the right decisions. But I will say that gathering all that information, and taking all of it into account, usually enabled me to make the best possible decision at the time.

The law of unintended consequences. I actually debated for some time where exactly to put this section in the book. But ultimately I decided it belongs here. Because a personal pet peeve of mine, for years, has been the fact that leaders all too often fail to take into account the possible long-term consequences of their decisions. Even the best-intentioned policies can sometimes have negative and completely unforeseen repercussions. Yet in many cases those could have been anticipated had the policy-makers taken the time to think things through. Doing so is an integral part of situational analysis and often involves information gathering, as well. To put it bluntly, no decision-making process is complete without a thorough consideration of the law of unintended consequences.

In 2015, Cecil the Lion was killed in Zimbabwe by an American big-game hunter. Long a major attraction at the Hwange National Park and therefore a kind of minor celebrity, Cecil was apparently taken legally outside the park, and the hunter was not prosecuted for poaching. Yet the international outrage that followed led to a number of restrictions on big-game hunting in Zimbabwe and elsewhere in Africa. The result was that, within a few months, park officials reported that a growing lion population constituted a threat to other animals and even humans, and that as many as two hundred lions would need to be "culled" by rangers, according to the *UK Telegraph*. Meanwhile, Zimbabwe lost millions in revenue they might have gleaned from the lucrative big-game-hunting business. Whereas wealthy hunters would have paid handsomely for the privilege of killing those two hundred lions, now officials not only had to cull the lion population themselves, but they had to pay people to do it.

Is big-game hunting moral? Should a nation profit from such a practice? Are there better ways to enact practical conservation measures? Those are all questions worth asking and thinking about. But a knee-jerk reaction, in this case, probably created more problems than it solved. Moreover, those problems probably should have been foreseen. That's the law of unintended consequences. Leaders and other decision-makers must constantly be asking themselves, as they consider solutions to problems, "If I do this, what else might happen down the road? Would that be better or worse than the current situation?"

Decision making. All of which brings us, finally, to decision making, which is the culmination of everything we've been talking about in this chapter up to this point. After all, solving problems entails something more than merely deciding what WOULD solve the problem. You have to take the next step and make a decision designed to actually solve the problem. Please note that this is explicitly a leadership skill. I mention that because I assume all of you reading this book will eventually find yourselves in leadership positions, if you're not already—especially if you follow the principles outlined here. Nothing says "leadership material" like the ability to think critically.

Tied up in the decision-making process are two other salient, journalism-type questions—namely, "Who will make the decision?" and "How will it be made?" The answer to "who" might be just you personally, or it might be a group. It depends on the situation, on the decision itself, and sometimes on the organization. A decision that involves just you, like where you're going to grad school or which job you're going to take, is ultimately yours and yours alone. (Unless you have a partner who will be directly affected by it. Then I highly recommend giving that person a vote.) But even if you have to make the decision alone, I still strongly advise that you seek advice from people who are knowledgeable about the subject matter or have personal experience with it. You might also "do your homework," which goes back to our point about research, above.

However, leaders often have to make decisions that affect a lot more people than just themselves. That's kind of the definition of leadership. In those situations, leaders are well advised to allow and encourage others who have a stake in the outcome to take part in the decision-making process. Often, this happens naturally, as individuals serve on committees, councils, or other representative bodies where decisions are made collectively. But sometimes, leaders have to go out of their way to make sure other people have a say—seeking their input, placing them in positions where they can have an impact, and creating a climate where people feel empowered to speak up without fear of retribution. This is known as "collegiality" or "consensus-building," and it is an excellent way to make many (most?) organizational decisions, because it captures the collective wisdom of the group.

When group decisions are called for, leaders can show, well, *leadership* by modeling critical thinking, sharing their thought processes and conclusions in a nonthreatening way, and encouraging others to do the same. My experience with committee meetings, for example (and believe me, I have A LOT of experience with committee meetings), has been that they can quickly get off track and become dominated by emotional factors or else devolve into discussions of irrelevant topics. But when the person leading the meeting has a clear plan (or "agenda," in the best sense of that term) and is able to keep everyone else focused on the issue at hand, while modeling objectivity and dispassionate analysis (but not in a robotic way), then the meeting is likely to be productive, as others follow that person's lead. Most people are quite capable of thinking critically; they just might need someone to remind them how.

And then there are, on (hopefully) rare occasions, decisions that a leader has to make unilaterally. Perhaps it's something that simply falls to the leader because of his or her position, like the decision to fire someone. After analyzing the situation, gathering all the relevant information, and talking to anyone who might have a relevant perspective, the leader simply has to make the final call. You've probably heard the old saying, "the buck stops here," usually attributed to President Harry Truman. Sometimes it does. Sometimes, as a leader, you just have to make the decision and take responsibility for it. That, too, is an integral part of leadership.

But it doesn't mean you have to flip a coin. Using all the elements of critical thinking that we've talked about in the last two chapters, you ought to be able to make the right decision most of the time. (No one makes the right decision all the time.) In fact, if you become really good at this whole critical thinking thing—remembering that most people, unfortunately, aren't very good at it, left to their own devices—you might actually gain a reputation for wisdom, as someone whose judgment is to be trusted. That's a pretty nice reputation to have.

Persuasion

The last practical application of critical thinking that I'd like to talk about in this chapter is persuasive writing and speaking. I'm actually not going to talk about it very much, at this point, because I plan to spend a couple of chapters on the topic of persuasion later in this book. (That's the "write better" part of the book; we're still on the "think better" part.) But I do want to at least introduce it here, briefly, in connection with critical thinking. Because the truth is, in the end, it doesn't matter how well you've analyzed the situation, how thoroughly you've researched it, or how well you've thought things through. If you can't communicate all of that clearly to someone else, it might as well not have happened.

That's something I tried to teach my students back when I taught technical writing in the college of engineering at a large research university. You think *you* don't want to be in this class? Imagine those guys (I use the term "guys" generically, but they were, back then, mostly guys). There they were, juniors or seniors, engineering majors, and they were having to take an "English class," as they saw it. Their body language on the first day of class—leaning back in their chairs, arms folded across their chests—said it all: "I'm going to be an engineer. Why do I need to be able to write?"

Oh, I don't know. Let's explore that question for a moment. Let's say you're a brilliant young engineer who's just been hired at a major firm. And in your first week on the job, because you're so brilliant, you come up with a plan for streamlining a certain process, perhaps solving a problem that has long perplexed more experienced engineers. So now, what are you going to do with that idea? Are you going to take the elevator up to the top floor, march into the CEO's office, put your feet up on her desk, and say, "You know, Sally, I was thinking . . . ."

No. Of course not. You're going to write that idea down in the form of a report and pass it on to your supervisor (who, if you're not careful, and if it really is a brilliant idea, will probably try to take credit for it, but let's leave that aside for a moment). And ask yourself this: From the moment you put that idea down on paper, which is more important—the initial brilliance of the idea itself, or how well you were able to explain and argue for it in writing?

The answer is obvious: In the end, it doesn't matter how good the idea is if you can't persuade someone else that it's a good idea. And that truism illustrates the importance of persuasion as an aspect of the critical thinking process—the culmination of that process, if you will. That doesn't mean the thinking piece itself is not important, or that persuasion is simply some kind of rhetorical sleight of hand, completely separate from reason and logic. As we will see in subsequent chapters, the two are closely tied together: Effective persuasion relies on and flows naturally out of efficient critical thinking. There are, to be sure, some excellent, time-tested rhetorical "tricks," or strategies, many of which we will cover. But those are morally and intellectually bankrupt if not based on the gold standard of critical thinking.

Meanwhile, you now know how to use your critical thinking skills to manage your time better; to figure out what's going on in a given situation (so you can decide what to do); to research and gather information; to make decisions; and to communicate those decisions and the reasons behind them to others, so they buy in. Not a bad day's work, for one chapter.

REFERENCE

Thornycroft, Peta. "'Cecil Effect' Leaves Park's Lions at Risk of Cull," *telegraph. co.uk*, *The Telegraph*, 20 February 2016.

WHAT IT MEANS TO WRITE WELL—AND WHY YOU SHOULD CARE

This is the point where we begin to make the shift from talking about thinking to talking about writing. Rest assured, though, that because the two are so thoroughly intertwined, we will not be able to escape the concept of critical thinking even as we turn our focus to writing—just as, in the last chapter, we couldn't help mentioning writing, as it relates to persuasion, even though our topic was ostensibly thinking. That will be especially true when we get into the chapter on using logic and reason to make arguments.

In this chapter, however, before we go on to talk about "good writing," I want to take some time to explain what I mean by that term and how it's relevant to you. In fact, let me tackle the last part of that equation, the relevancy question, first. Why should you care about learning to write well? What's in it for you?

A Few Assumptions

Whenever I talk to a group of college students or young adults about writing, I always begin with certain assumptions. If you're in college, for example, I assume that you plan to earn a college degree. Further, I assume that the reason you want a college degree is probably not for personal enrichment (no offense) but because you hope, eventually, to land the kind of high-paying, professional job that requires a college degree. If you've already graduated from college, and you already have that coveted job, then I assume you have a desire to be highly successful at it and move "up the ladder," as they say, within your field.

Do those seem like reasonable assumptions?

I don't assume, by the way, that very many people in my audience (perhaps not any) are planning to become professional writers. In all my years of teaching college writing, I've had only a handful of students who wanted to be writers. Obviously, that's true for corporate or nonprofit groups, as well. Those folks already have jobs, and very few if any include the word "writer" in their title—nor are they seeking such a job.

Perhaps I should note, to be fair, that this dynamic has evolved somewhat over the last decade or so due to the ubiquity of the Internet. Nowadays, anybody who wants to can have a blog, and lots of people do. Some of the young people I've taught in the last two or three years already have that in mind, even if they're not really studying to be "professional writers," per se. Some already have their own blogs. Others come to blogging later in life, when their college years are long behind them. (I bet they wish they'd paid more attention in their writing classes!) But for the most part, I think my observation holds true: Most of my students are not planning to become professional writers.

Yet here's the rub: You might not be planning to be a professional writer, but if you're going to be a professional—defined as someone with a college degree and a job that requires a college degree—then you're going to be a writer. In our information-dependent society, that's what professionals do: They communicate with each other. Some of that communication is interpersonal, just talking to each other in person or on the phone, and some of it may be verbal within a larger context, such as a meeting or conference. But the vast majority of professional communication these days is written, in the form of reports, proposals, prospectuses, letters, text messages, and—the biggie—e-mails.

(Just as an aside, I know a lot of young people regard e-mail as outdated, as just the way us "old folks" communicate. There may be some truth to that. E-mail may eventually become passé. For now, though, it is still the primary way that professionals communicate with each other in writing. And by the way, in most industries, it's the people who have been there for a while—aka, the "old folks"— who are running things. You definitely want to be able to communicate with them in the way they prefer. That's why it's important for you to know how to write effective e-mails—important enough that I've devoted an entire chapter to the topic at the end of this book.)

Fry Cook No More

What I said above about communication is true regardless of the field you're in. Health care, education, business management, engineering—it doesn't matter. As management guru Peter Drucker noted long ago, the one skill that all employees must have is the ability to communicate effectively. To put it another way, in our modern-day business culture, the minute you rise one step above fry cook, writing becomes part of your job.

Here's what I mean by that. Let's say you're a fry cook at a local fast-food restaurant. One day the store manager offers you a job as an assistant manager. You accept, because it means more money. Now, all of a sudden, you find that part of your job involves sitting the office, doing "paperwork"—which is really just another name for writing. (Yes, some of it may be computation, working with numbers, but most of it is just plain, old-fashioned report writing.)

If you're successful and one day become store manager, you'll be doing even more writing. And even more if you rise to the level of district manager—all the way up the ladder, until you finally become CEO, at which point you can probably hire somebody to do your writing for you. But right up to that point, as your career progresses, effective writing becomes more and more important.

There's an inverse relationship between writing and advancement, too: The better you are at communicating, both in speaking and (especially) in writing, the faster you're likely to climb the ladder, and the higher you're likely to climb. One of my sons was considering going into accounting, but he wasn't sure he wanted to spend his days adding up rows of numbers. A good friend of our family, a guy who became a partner at one of the Big Four accounting firms about five years ahead of schedule, told him, "It's not really about numbers. We have programs that can do that. The reason I'm one of the youngest accountants ever to make partner at my firm is because I know how to communicate with people. I can talk to them, one on one, and I can write. That's what makes a great auditor. Anybody can add."

Indeed, such "soft skills" have become increasingly valuable in today's job market. Having the ability to write well, in addition to all the other skills people in your profession need, can certainly help you land a job, or a better job than the one you have now; and once you're in that job, those same skills will undoubtedly help you succeed and move up. (Remember the engineering students I talked about in the last chapter?)

So my advice would be to take advantage of this opportunity—reading this book, taking this course or seminar—to learn all you can about writing. Work to improve yourself as a writer. Don't think of it as "language arts" or "English" or whatever you've gotten used to calling it. The only thing it has to do with English is that's the language we use. If we were all living in Italy and speaking Italian, I would be talking about pretty much exactly the same things. This is about communicating effectively, about writing well. What that means, we'll see in the next section.

What is "good writing"?

As soon as I utter the phrase "good writing," a lot of my students start to roll their eyes and tune me out. They've heard it all before from their previous teachers. Yeah, yeah, you need to be able to use good grammar. And then there are all those stories and poems and essays by famous writers—why can't you guys write something like that?

Well, that's not exactly what I mean when I say "good writing." Of course we admire those great writers and wish we had their skill, in much the same way we admire great musicians or athletes. Of course using good grammar (or rather, using Standard English well) is important, as we'll see in a later chapter. But for our purposes, at this point in the discussion, when I say "good writing," I'm really talking about three things.

Making yourself clearly understood. In professional writing (i.e., the writing you do as part of your job), this is the single most important thing. Perhaps you're thinking to yourself, "Well, duh, of course people should be able to understand you." And you're right—it ought to be a given. Sadly, it isn't. Making themselves clearly understood in a piece of writing is something that, apparently, a lot of people can't do, or at least don't bother to do. (I'm tempted to say "most people," but I hope that's not true—although I fear it is.) This is evident from the surveys we looked at back in Chapter 1, where employers consistently complain that the young people they're hiring right out of college can't write. I think this is what they mean: that those young people can't compose a clear report or letter or e-mail.

And if that isn't enough evidence, just try reading your car insurance policy. Or your latest bank statement. Or your political science textbook. Recent college graduates aren't the only culprits. This problem has been around for a long time, and it affects a lot of people—perhaps most.

Part of the problem, I think, is what I alluded to above—that most reasonably well-educated people might have the ability to write clearly, if they actually tried, but they don't bother. They're a little lazy, or they're just going through the motions, or they think it doesn't matter. It's kind of like what we talked about in earlier chapters, in relation to thinking. Most people are plenty smart enough to think critically, and they may even have acquired some of the skills along the way. Much of it is intuitive, in any case. They just don't bother taking the time. They don't even try. The same is true with writing clearly—which is, by the way, a natural by-product of thinking clearly. Again, the two go hand-in-hand, which is why I devoted the first four chapters to thinking before we even got to writing. And just as you can set yourself apart from the competition merely by making an effort to think critically, you can also set yourself apart simply by making a concerted effort to write clearly. (Again, in both cases, it helps if you have the requisite skills. But that's what this book is for.)

The other part of the problem, though, is that shoddy writing (and thinking) is often rewarded in our society, or at least not penalized. Students go through school reading poorly written textbooks, and then they get into the professional world and find (if they notice it at all) that most of the stuff they're reading there is also pretty bad, and some of it virtually unreadable. They naturally assume that's just the way of the world—bad writing is the norm, apparently, and no one really cares if you write well or not. (Except maybe an English teacher or two—but who listens to them?)

It's actually worse than that, though. Because the truth is, the clarity of any piece of writing in our culture tends to be inversely proportional to the education level of its writer. In other words, the more education people get, the worse they tend to write, or at least the less clear they tend to be. Would you rather ask directions from some random person on the street, or from someone with an Ivy League PhD? Chances are, the directions you'd get from the PhD would be so convoluted, so full of polysyllabic words and punctuated with interrupters and qualifiers, that you'd probably get yourself good and lost.

But students spend so much time reading textbooks and scholarly articles written that way, and listening to their professors talk that way, that they conclude it must just be the way educated people talk (or write). And so, wishing to appear educated, they imitate that style and therefore become, themselves, unintelligible. That's such a significant problem that I'm going to devote an entire chapter to it, later.

But there's one more danger I want to mention before I move on: Not all of what I've described above is unintentional. What the really smart people learn from all the jargon-laden inflated prose they encounter in college is that, if you want people to think you're smart, that's the way to go about it. The heck with anyone actually understanding you: The important thing is that they're impressed with your brilliance. In other words, smart people all too often use language to build barriers, to say, "Look how smart I am" or even, "I'm much smarter than you—no wonder you can't understand me!" And yet the true purpose of communicating ought to be building bridges of understanding. Ultimately, if people can't understand you, what's the point? What are you accomplishing?

We'll talk more, in a later chapter, about how to develop a clear writing style. At this point, I just want to establish that when I talk about "good writing," the first thing I mean is that you can write clearly, in a way that readers can actually understand.

Putting your best foot forward. The second thing I mean, when I talk about "good writing," is writing in such a way that people will make positive assumptions about you, not negative assumptions—that they will judge you to be intelligent, well-educated, and competent, rather than the opposite of those things.

Because, let's be honest, people WILL judge you based on the way you write. As human beings, we're constantly judging other people based on any number of things: height, weight, clothing, skin color, accent—you name it. That's not a very attractive feature of human nature, but it is a feature nonetheless. Obviously, we should try to avoid judging people based on such factors, but we can't just pretend it doesn't happen. And we can't ignore the fact that, in a professional context, people will judge us based on what they perceive to be our level of professionalism.

A good friend of mine grew up in a very small town in the Deep South. He's a sharp guy—smart, well-educated, accomplished—with an impressive résumé. Unfortunately for him, he used to have a thick Southern drawl. All too often, other educated professionals assumed that he must be a stupid redneck, simply because he sounded like their idea of a stupid redneck. His accent became such a professional handicap that he actually went back to college and took elocution classes in the drama department to mitigate it (which helped, by the way). The people who judged him harshly because of the way he spoke were wrong. But that didn't stop them from doing it.

The same thing happens when people read something we write. They decide, based on what and how we've written, if we're smart. If we're well-educated. If we know what we're talking about. Whether (and this is key) they want to do business with us. Those judgments might be unfair. Their conclusions might be wrong. But that won't prevent them from making flawed assumptions or arriving at faulty conclusions.

And by the way, let's not forget that in modern professional life, you're likely to be communicating via e-mail with people you don't know well, or perhaps don't know at all. They may be on another floor of your building, where you run into them occasionally in the hallway or a meeting. They may work for a branch in another city, so that you've only met them once or twice. Or they may work for another organization on the other side of the country, and you never meet them at all—or rather, they never get to meet you and find out what a warm, smart, wonderful person you are. All they know about you is what they read.

Another brief story: Several years ago, as interest rates fell, I began thinking about refinancing my home. So I went to a popular Web site that shares information with lenders, entered my data, and waited for banks to contact me. By the following day, I'd heard from four, offering different rates and terms. I picked the one that looked best and asked for more information. Later that day I received a reply from a young bank employee offering further details. Actually, I have no idea if she was young. I just assumed she was because her long e-mail was full of emoticons and text-messaging abbreviations—including, I kid you not, "LOL." You can probably imagine what I was thinking at that point: "Why did I get the fourteen-year-old loan officer? Can I have one of the thirty-five-year-olds, please?"

I confess that I judged her rather harshly because of the way she communicated—her use of language. That might not have been fair or accurate. For all I know, she might have been forty-two years old. Or she might have just graduated summa cum laude from Stanford. But I couldn't help being put off. I also didn't do business with that bank.

When people graduate from college and start looking for a job, they usually go out and buy a new suit to wear to interviews—even if they were the kind of people who, in college, always wore tee shirts and flip-flops. Why? Because they "want to make a good first impression." But the truth is, showing up for the interview in their new suit does NOT constitute their first impression. Chances are, that interviewer read something they wrote—an e-mail, a resume, a cover letter—long before laying eyes on them and has already formed a first impression—which is why they got the interview to begin with. That's how important writing can be.

The power of persuasion. Ultimately, in professional life, the purpose of writing is to get people to do what you want them to do. In saying that, I don't mean to sound overly cynical. It's nice to think that the purpose of writing is to fulfill some inner desire to express yourself, or to pursue truth, or some other high-sounding goal. And in another context, those things might be true. But when it comes to writing as part of your job, the goal is to get people to do things: invite you for an interview, hire you, buy your product or service, adopt your proposal, follow your directions. The extent to which you can get people to do those things will largely determine your professional success. And the way we do it is often through writing.

Remember, in the very first Star Wars movie, back in 1977, the scene in which Obi Wan Kenobi waves his hand at a couple of Storm Troopers and says, "These are not the droids you were looking for?" Ever wished you could do that when you were a teenager? You come dragging home at 2:30 a.m., and your mom is sitting there on the couch, arms folded across her chest, tapping her foot, so you wave your hand in front of her and say, "It's 11:30." Wouldn't that be nice?

Of course, we don't have that power. But to the extent that we have anything remotely like it, the power lies in our ability to persuade people—verbally and, most of all, in writing. That's such an important aspect of "good writing" that, again, I've devoted an entire chapter to it later in this book. For now, though, I just want you to understand where we're headed with all this. Good writing, for working professionals, is not something esoteric or artsy. It's all about advancing your agenda.

So that's what I mean by "writing well": making yourself clearly understood, making a good impression on readers (or at least not a bad impression), and ultimately being able to persuade them. Next, I want to talk a little bit about the writing process—how we actually produce a piece of writing—and about what constitutes a good writing style. Then we'll go on to discuss how to use logic and reason (i.e., critical thinking) to make effective arguments in writing.

THE WRITING PROCESS

I clearly remember sitting in my first-year writing course as an eighteen-year-old college student, listening to the professor drone on about writing. (Perhaps you can relate.) We had two textbooks in the course, a thick grammar handbook and a collection of essays by well-known, talented professional writers. The professor's basic premise seemed to be that, if we just devoted ourselves to memorizing the grammar handbook, then we would eventually be able to write essays like the ones in the book.

I remember thinking, "Well, that would be nice. I would love to write something like that. For one thing, I'd definitely make an A in this stupid class. And I'd also enjoy it. It would be very satisfying to be able to write like that." The question I couldn't escape, though, was "how?" How did I write something as good as one of those professional essays?

And don't tell me the answer is "by learning grammar," which seemed to be my professor's default position. That's kind of like saying if you want to learn to drive, you have to memorize the driver's manual. No one denies that, for drivers, knowing what's in the manual is a good thing, or that it will help you be a better driver once you're behind the wheel. But learning the "rules of the road" by itself does not enable anyone to drive. Learning to drive takes more than just reading a book.

I actually learned that the hard way when I was in high school. In those days, driver's education was an actual class that we took during the school day—basically, it was a way of hiring an additional assistant football coach. (But I digress.) In fact, it was a year-long class, where we spent the first semester in the classroom, reading texts (like the state driver's manual), watching films, and memorizing pieces of information. The second semester is when we actually got in the car, along with the instructor, and headed out on the open road. Well, we headed out to the school parking lot first, but eventually we hit the open road.

For me, that first semester was a breeze. Reading and memorizing stuff? Taking multiple choice tests? No sweat. I could do that in my sleep (and sometimes did). I aced everything and made an A in the first part of the class. There was only one problem.

I couldn't drive.

That became painfully evident the first time we got in the car, not long after we came back from the holiday break. Literally everyone in the class knew how to drive except me, because they had all driven a car before, whereas I hadn't. I grew up in a pretty rural part of the country, where it wasn't at all unusual for kids to learn to drive on country roads at age eleven or twelve. But I was a "city kid" (comparatively), and my parents weren't about to let me drive around our small suburban neighborhood without a license. The first time I got behind the wheel of that driver's ed car was the first time I'd ever been behind the wheel—and it showed. Kids who had barely passed the first semester were gliding down the road at sixty-five meter per hour, whereas I couldn't even get out of the parking lot.

My point is that, if you want to learn to drive a car, you have to spend significant time actually driving a car. Just reading the manual isn't enough—although it sure helps once you get out in traffic and start trying to coexist safely with other drivers. Likewise, if you want to improve your writing, you have to spend a significant amount of time writing. Just memorizing the grammar handbook isn't enough. Of course it's important to be able to use Standard English well if you want to successfully reach your readers—important enough that I talk about it, at length, elsewhere in this book. But writing isn't solely, or even primarily, about grammar.

Which brings me back to the "how" I mentioned above.

How Do Writers Write?

If you want to learn how to do something, it makes sense to ask people who already know how to do it—like getting your mom or dad to teach you to drive in an empty parking lot, back when you were fifteen. The same is true of writing: Instead of just asking, "How do I write a good essay (or report or whatever)?" it makes sense to ask, "How do actual writers do it?"

If we assume writers have some special ability the rest of us don't have, then asking them how they do it doesn't make any sense. That would be like a Muggle asking Albus Dumbledore how to do magic. I assure you, however, that's not the case. Writers don't have special, magical abilities. Mostly, they just know things about writing that most people don't know, partly because they've been taught, perhaps, but mostly because they just do it so much. They've learned from experience. And if we start with that assumption—that writers are just regular people who know how to do something the rest of us don't know how to do—then it makes perfect sense to ask them how they do it.

Back in the 1960s, several researchers decided to do just that. They were college writing instructors who were regularly attending conferences and having conversations with colleagues about how they could help students improve their writing. Eventually, a few of them came up with what I've always thought was an extremely sensible idea—much more sensible than we might expect from college professors. Instead of sitting around in their ivory towers theorizing about how to write, they decided, they would ask actual writers how THEY do it.

So they did. By various means, they began studying how writers write. Now, when I say "writers," what you probably picture are novelists, playwrights, poets—people like that. And they certainly included those in their inquiries. But the majority of the people they studied were just everyday, working writers—people who went in to work every morning, just like the rest of us, but what they did all day was write. People like journalists, copywriters, and technical writers. Basically, the researchers were looking for answers to very simple questions: From the time those folks began a writing project, however they defined "beginning" (whether the project was assigned to them or they came up with it on their own) to the time they finished, however they defined that (turning it in to their boss or sending it to their editor or whatever)—between those two points, what exactly did they do and how much time do they spend on each step, expressed as a percentage of the whole?

In a relatively short period of time, they were able to collect a great deal of data, and as they began culling through that data, something truly remarkable began to emerge. But before I tell you what it was, let me share something I believe about human nature. I'm convinced that most people, faced with a repetitive task, will initially experiment with various ways of accomplishing that task until they hit on the way that is most efficient, meaning it produces the desired result in the least amount of time. The first time I ever unloaded the dishwasher in our current house, it took me fifteen minutes. But I kept experimenting with the best way to do it—dealing with the plates first, then moving on to the glasses, or vice-versa—until I got my unloading time down to five minutes. Now I do it the same way every time.

For most of the people who took part in these surveys, writing was a repetitive task, something they had to do day in and day out. Just like anybody else, they were looking for the most efficient way to do it. They had to do a good job on each project if they wanted to keep their job; but at the same time, they couldn't afford to take forever while work piled up in their inbox. It doesn't make sense that they would go out of their way to make things harder for themselves. On the contrary, just like you or me, they would try to figure out the easiest way of doing the job well.

The remarkable thing is that, when it came to explaining how they went about writing, virtually all of those folks, from all over the country, individually and independently of each other (it's not like they knew each other), came up with essentially the same approach. And that is what we refer to today as "the writing process."

Process versus Product

"The writing process" is a term you may be familiar with from high-school or other college-level courses. However, I'm going to take some time to go over it in this chapter because, in my experience, most people don't really know what it means. It has become a popular educational buzz-phrase, kind of like "critical thinking," but at least half the people using it don't seem to know what process they're talking about.

In order to better understand the term, it might be useful to recognize its opposite. Remember when I talked about my first-year college writing course, back at the beginning of this chapter? Where the professor had two textbooks, a grammar handbook and a collection of essays, and implied that our job was to memorize the first and then imitate the second? That's actually an age-old strategy for teaching writing known as the "product approach." It's the way writing was taught in this country (and elsewhere) for many years. In fact, it's the very approach those researchers were questioning when they decided to go to the source and find out how real writers write.

The problem with the product approach, for people trying to improve their writing, is that it focuses completely on the "what"—what a piece of writing should look like when it's finished. In other words, the product. Not that the product isn't important. Of course it is. In the end, that's all we have to judge by. But the real issue for writers, especially at the beginning stages, isn't the "what"—it's the "how." Yes, we know what a piece of writing ought to look like when it's finished—we've read all those professional essays, thank you very much—but HOW do we make it look and sound like that?

The answer to that question—the "how" question—is the writing process, the process through which writers work to create a piece of writing. And that process is what began to emerge as the researchers culled through all the data they had gathered. I said that what they saw was remarkable, and it was. Because what they found was that virtually all the respondents were describing to them the same basic process.

So What Is the Writing Process?

What those researchers found is that basically all writers do essentially the same things, with minor variations. First, they spend a great deal of time figuring out what, exactly, they're trying to say—as much as sixty percent of their total project time, for many of them. That's the stage of the writing process we sometimes refer to as "pre-writing," although I'm not a big fan of that term, as you'll see in a moment. Next, once they have a pretty good idea of what they want to say, they set out to say it in what we call a "draft," or a first attempt. Then they go back to that draft and start figuring out ways to improve it—not just correcting errors and other flaws, but actually making it a better piece of writing. We call that third stage "editing and revising."

Invention. As I said, I don't care much for the term "pre-writing." It implies that this stage of the process is somehow previous to, and therefore not altogether part of, the writing itself. But of course that isn't true. This first stage is an integral and indispensable part of the overall process. On a very basic level, if what we mean by "writing" is "putting words on the page," then you had darn well better be putting words on the page at this stage of the process, for a couple of reasons.

First, if the purpose of "pre-writing" is to gather ideas and information for whatever you're writing, then as a practical matter you need to be keeping a record of those things—and that means writing them down. How many times have you had a good idea about a project while driving home from school or work, but by the time you got to a point where you could write it down, it had flown out of your head, never to return? We all understand intuitively that, if you don't write things down, in a very real sense, you don't have them.

Second, the act of writing is itself generative, meaning that it generates ideas. As you jot down your ideas, you tend to get additional ideas. I'm not a psychologist, so I can't explain exactly how this works or why it works, but I can attest that it does—especially if you're not too worried, at that early stage, about grammar, punctuation, spelling, and so forth. (Not that those things aren't important. They're just things to be concerned about later in the process.)

So no, this stage of the writing process isn't "pre" anything. It's part of the process—which is why I prefer the term "invention," coined by Aristotle many years ago. I like the way "invention" suggests the creative nature of the enterprise. We like to draw a distinction between "creative writing" and . . . what? Noncreative writing? ALL writing is creative; the act of filling the page with words is itself an act of creation. I think "invention" captures that dynamic quite nicely.

Invention, then, is the "gathering ideas stage," as I put it above. Gathering them from where? Well, that depends. There are lots of places to get ideas, starting with your own head. And I mean "starting with" literally, because that's where you should always start—with what you already know about your topic. To access that information, you can use a strategy like free writing or brainstorming, which will also help you understand what I meant when I said that writing is generative. Jotting down your thoughts quickly, without editing or self-censorship ("I can't say that!"), will literally give you more ideas, ultimately leading you to dredge up thoughts you didn't even know were in your head.

Even so, depending on what you're writing about, the information you already have will rarely be enough to cover the topic adequately. You're probably going to have to do some type of research—and I'm not just talking about going to the college library (or its virtual equivalent). If you're writing a report for your boss, you're doubtless going to spend a great deal of time on the company databases, finding the information you need. If you're looking for a new vendor, or putting together an e-mail marketing list, or trying to choose a health plan—well, you get the picture. We talked about the importance of research back in Chapter 3, as an integral part of the thinking process. Now we see that it's also an integral part of the writing process. Funny how that works, huh?

Before we move on, let me say one more thing about invention. Did you notice what I said above—that, on average, writers spend about 50 to 60 percent of their total project time at this stage? You might be thinking to yourself, "That seems a little excessive." Perhaps you're even thinking you can cut down on the time it takes to complete a project simply by skipping this stage, or at least greatly curtailing it.

Don't try it. It doesn't work. When I say the invention stage is integral to the process, I mean just that. It's important. It's beyond important—it's indispensable. What you'll find, as you devote the necessary time and effort to this stage, is that doing so ultimately does not increase your time on task—it actually decreases your time AND the amount of work required, by providing all the information you need to complete your project. After all, how much of your "writing" time do you actually spend staring off into space, wondering what to say next? Effective invention practically eliminates that wasted time, making the process both easier and faster. That's why professional writers spend so much time on this stage—because, remember, they're not trying to make things harder on themselves. Quite the opposite.

Drafting. The next thing our researchers discovered is that, after spending a significant amount of time figuring what they want to say, writers then try to say it. We refer to this activity as "drafting."

When I say drafting, what I'm describing is the activity you probably think of when I use the word "writing": putting words together to form sentences, sentences together to create paragraphs, and paragraphs together to make essays. That's what I call drafting. "Writing," for me (or for any writer), is the entire process, including invention and editing (which we'll get to in a moment). Drafting means that you take all the information you gathered during the invention stage, which is probably pretty jumbled and disorganized, and start pulling it together into something that kind of, sort of, almost looks a little bit like the finished product. In other words, a draft is nothing more than an attempt to turn ideas into a piece of writing that someone else can read and understand—and your very first attempt is what we call the "first draft."

That first draft will rarely be very good. In fact, that's kind of the definition of a first draft. No one expects it to be very good—much less perfect—and you shouldn't, either. It's a draft, for heaven's sake. A first attempt. In fact, one of the worst things you can do as a writer is try too hard to make that first draft perfect. For one thing, it's not going to be perfect, no matter how hard you try. Plus, spending that much time and effort trying to edit as you go is generally counterproductive. At this stage, attempting to say things perfectly will probably just prevent you from saying anything at all. To be sure, drafting takes your writing a step beyond invention strategies like free writing or brainstorming, yet it has something important in common with both: It's vital, at this point, just to write, to get words on the page, and not worry too much about how good or well-organized they are. That comes later.

Personally, I tend to sort of semi-free write my first draft of an essay (or section of a book, or whatever). That is, I'll spend some time figuring out what I want to say, including talking to people or doing research as needed, and then at some point I'll just sit down and try to say it. Along the way, I don't spend much time worrying about whether I've used exactly the right words or if my sentences are as smooth as I'd like. I can deal with that later. At this stage, I'm just trying to get my basic ideas on paper, in a form I can work with.

Sometimes, as I'm doing this, I'll hear a little voice inside my head saying things like, "This is garbage. You call yourself a writer?" The temptation just to trash everything and start over can be overwhelming. I simply resist it. I've come up with a little mantra that I recite to myself in those cases: "It's just a draft. It's just a draft. It's just a draft." That helps me stay focused and crank out the pages. And once I have a draft, however rough it might be, I find that I feel a lot better about the project, overall.

Which brings us to the third and final stage of the writing process:

Editing. So your first draft isn't very good. So what? You can always fix it. That's the true beauty of the writing process, as our intrepid researchers learned from their subjects. A draft is just that—a draft. An attempt. It's not the final version.

The "fixing it" part is what we call "editing," or to be more precise, "editing and revising." Editing involves going through a draft and figuring out how to make it better. Note that the purpose of editing is not simply to fix mistakes. There will probably be plenty of those, for sure, especially as you're going through the learning process and mastering Standard English (more to come on that topic). Even experienced writers, who might not make many technical or grammatical errors, still have to worry about typos and such. So "fixing" problems and correcting mistakes is certainly a part of the editing process.

But it's not the only part. It's not really even the most important part, or at least it becomes less important as you become a more proficient writer and make fewer of those kinds of mistakes. Editing is really about making the piece of writing better, which goes far beyond just fixing errors. It involves looking closely at every word to make sure it's the right word, the word you wanted in that context. It means looking at every single sentence to make sure they're all the best, strongest sentences you can write, under the circumstances—and that they all fit together logically and flow smoothly. Often, editing requires you to go back to what you were originally trying to say and make sure, as you read through your draft, that you've said it, and said it clearly in a way people can understand and follow.

"Revising" refers to actually making changes. Editing is deciding what changes to make, and revising is making them. And once you're done making all the changes you decided to make to your essay (or report, or whatever), you have . . . you guessed it! Another draft! And then what do you do? Why, you go back and edit that draft, decide what still needs some work, make the necessary changes, and produce another draft, over and over again in a cycle of drafting, editing, revising, editing some more, revising some more, and so on. Every now and then, you may find yourself going back up to the invention stage, because you realize you didn't really think something through or you don't have enough information. But mostly it's a cycle of drafting and revising.

How many drafts? That depends on a number of factors: the importance of what you're writing, its length, your deadline, and your own personality, among others. But several drafts, at least. It's hard to say exactly how many drafts I write, since I'm editing and revising on the screen, but if I printed out the document after each time I went through it and made changes, I'd estimate that I typically write five or six drafts, which is pretty average for a professional writer. Most of the time, the biggest changes come as I move from the first draft to the second; after that, I'm mostly fine-tuning and tightening my sentences (something we'll talk about in the chapter on writing style). But I've been known to go back, even after multiple drafts, and make significant changes to the organization, or add a lot more information, or even make drastic cuts.

And that's fine. In fact, it's precisely the point. That's what drafts are for: to give you, as writer, a chance to figure out what the piece is lacking and make it better, stronger, more detailed, and clearer—not to mention more correct. Because even though that might not be the main focus of editing, "fixing" grammar, punctuation, and typos is certainly an important task. The writing process, as we saw back at the beginning of this chapter, is not just about the product; it's about how to get to that product. Yet, in the end, all you have is a product, a piece of writing, and that is what readers will ultimately judge you by.

Three Big Take-Aways

From all this discussion about the writing process, we can, I think, learn three very important lessons. The first is that you can't make something out of nothing. Even the best of artists don't pull their creations out of thin air. The sculptor needs his granite. The painter needs her canvass and colors. The writer needs words and ideas.

Unfortunately, plenty of people, perhaps most, make the common mistake of trying to write something without having put any thought or research or preparation into what they want to say. They're trying just to pull a piece of writing out of thin air, and it doesn't work. That's one of the main reasons most people find writing such a difficult task. They sit down to write something, and the words just won't come, and they wonder why. Well, maybe it's because they haven't put any effort into figuring out what to say. No wonder they can't say anything!

The second key take-away is that a piece of writing never comes out right the first time—and probably not the second or third, either. Maybe not even the sixth or seventh. That's perfectly normal. It's not a reflection on your intelligence or writing ability. It's just the way it is. The secret to good writing, if there is a secret, is multiple drafts. That was true for Shakespeare, it was true for Maya Angelou and J.K. Rowling, it's true for me, and it's true for you.

Perhaps some of you have read Leo Tolstoy's novel *War and Peace*, or at least seen a copy of it. It's about as thick as the New York City phone book used to be. (Anybody remember phone books?) What you might not know is that what we have today as *War and Peace* is actually Tolstoy's seventh draft of that novel. He wrote that manuscript over—by hand—seven times before he felt comfortable enough with it to send it to his publisher. Toward the end of his life, an interviewer asked him, "Dr. Tolstoy, do you ever go back and read your own novels?" To which he answered, "No, I can't bear to. All I see are the things I wish I could change."

THAT is how a writer thinks. A little OC, perhaps—well, okay, maybe a lot OC. I'm not necessarily trying to make you that obsessive about your writing. But I am trying to make you a little bit obsessive, or at least get you to think about writing differently, to see it as a process. I want you to recognize the importance of figuring out what you want to say before trying to say it and then working toward that goal through a series of drafts—all of which will make you not only a better and more effective writer, but a more efficient one, too.

Because the third key take-away is that the writing process, once mastered, does not make the task of writing more difficult or time-consuming. In fact, the opposite is true: Once you've stopped trying to edit and censor yourself at the very same time you're trying to write something, you'll be amazed at how much more smoothly your ideas flow and how much better they are. That's even truer for us, here in the twenty-first century, than it was for Leo Tolstoy, thanks to modern technology. The process remains the same: invention, drafting, and editing. But the actual work becomes much easier because, for instance, we don't have to write an entire draft over by hand in order to make corrections. We can write a draft on our word processor, go back and edit on the screen, then make whatever changes we need to make to the document and, *viola*! Another draft!

And so it goes, one draft after another, until the piece of writing is as good as it's going to be, as good as you can make it given your current skill level. Or maybe as good as you can make it, given your time constraints and other obligations. No piece of writing is ever going to be perfect—but you can certainly make it better.

So Just to Recap Briefly . . .

One of the main reasons most people don't write well is that they're trying to do too much at once. They're attempting to entertain too many variables in their head simultaneously. They want to have good ideas, have something worthwhile to say, and at the same time say it well, with all the right words arranged into strong sentences and logical paragraphs, while at the same time not making any grammatical errors or misspelling any words or getting their commas out of place, or—whew! That's a lot to remember. How do people do it?

The answer is, they don't. Nobody can control for that many variables all at once. Our minds don't work that way. Professional writers, as those pioneering researchers learned, are not people who can keep all those factors in mind at the same time, whereas the rest of us can't; they're people who have learned that they can't either, and so they've figured out a way to cope. A work-around. That's what we refer to as the writing process.

Basically, what the process does is to break things down. Instead of trying to come up with good ideas, AND write them down, AND do it perfectly in one sitting, the writing process divided those tasks into manageable pieces. First, you figure out what you want to say, without worrying at all about how you're going to say it. Then you try to say it, with a focus on getting your ideas onto the page—not on saying it particularly well. Then you go back and make sure you've said what you intended to say AND work on saying it in the best way possible.

That is the writing process in a nutshell. And learning to rely on that process consistently is what will enable you to be a more effective writer and arguer, both in the academic arena and as a career professional.

AVOIDING COMMON GRAMMATICAL MISTAKES (THAT EVEN THE PROS MAKE)

This is not a grammar handbook, nor was it meant to be. In fact, I don't really like to talk about grammar any more than I have to. The problem is, I usually have to. As an English professor, it's kind of an occupational hazard. More to the point, writers (and not just my students) are frequently guilty of making glaring grammatical errors that could easily be fixed if they just knew what they were doing. Often, as a teacher, corporate trainer, or editor, it's my job to point those things out to people and help them understand and fix the problem.

That's not merely obsessive, school-marmish behavior on my part. Remember what I said back in Chapter 5 about how people will judge you based on the way you write? That is absolutely true, and many of those judgments will stem from bad grammar. If you think English teachers are the only grammar Nazis, then you're probably in for a rude awakening.

Some years ago, I was walking across campus, minding my own business, when a professor in another department whom I barely knew marched up to me, clearly angry. Before I could say a word, he proceeded to berate me for several minutes because his students, according to him, were such poor writers, by which he meant they used bad grammar. Somehow, this was all my fault, because as an English professor I was supposed to fix all that before they got to him. So again—if you think it's only the English department that cares about grammar, you're sadly mistaken.

Specifically, what I'd like to do in this chapter is discuss a handful of common grammatical errors—and I mean literally a handful. We're talking about five specific errors that are so common that, as I say in the title of this chapter, even the pros struggle with them. These are the errors that I see constantly as a professional editor—like the time I was asked to edit my college's new catalog, for instance. That job consists primarily of taking documents written by lots of different people, from different departments, and organizing them into one coherent and much longer document. Basically, each unit of the university writes its own piece, and then the editor tries to pull them all together in such a way that they not only make sense but sound like they were all written by the same person.

That meant I was getting loads of documents all written by people with master's and doctoral degrees. And they were awful. The writing, I mean, not the people. It was awful. It contained the exact same errors that I see in my first-year writing students' papers and in roughly the same proportions. Honestly, that experience made me look at students' writing a little differently. How can we expect them to be perfect when their professors still struggle? But it also made me realize that I need to do a better job of addressing those issues, as early as possible. Because the truth is, I did tend to have a little less respect for some of my colleagues, once I saw how badly many of them wrote (even though they were supposed to know better). I don't want that same thing to happen to my students. That's why I think it's important to talk about the most common errors and how to avoid them.

What Is Grammar?

Before I go on and address those five grammatical errors, I'd like to spend a few minutes explaining what I mean when I use the word "grammar." We often think of grammar as the dictates of the Language Police, telling us what we can and can't say and how to say it. But that isn't really true. All languages evolve over time, based on the way people use them, and the English language is no exception. Just compare modern English, from any newspaper or magazine, to Shakespeare's English. Or even to a newspaper from fifty years ago.

The fact that language evolves, however, doesn't mean there aren't any guidelines. There are. We call them "grammar," otherwise known as the rules of Standard English. Perhaps I should add the word "American" to that phrase: "Standard American English," or SAE, because, of course, British English is a little different, and I've taught many students from places like Jamaica and South Africa, where the queen's English dominates.

The word "standard" in this context is not prescriptive. It does not refer to a flag we must all salute. Rather, it simply describes accepted norms—in this case, accepted in the workplace by college-educated professionals. As we noted above, language is constantly evolving, and today's norms are not the norms of 1850, or even 1950. Nevertheless, norms do exist, and educated people must generally abide by them if they are to communicate effectively.

That's why we have a standardized language in the first place. People grow up in different parts of the country, in different families and communities, speaking different versions or dialects of English—or not speaking English at all. The main purpose of language is to communicate, and if the language or dialect you use in a particular situation allows you to do that, then it is effective.

As I tell my students, English teachers are fond of using words like "wrong" and "error," but those words have meaning only as they apply to Standard English. In our personal lives—as we converse, text, or e-mail with friends and family—there is no "wrong" language. The problem is that, in our work lives, we frequently share documents or exchanging e-mails with people from other families, other parts of the country, and other walks of life. Assuming that all those people will understand the language or local dialect you grew up speaking only leads to confusion, misunderstanding, and false impressions—all of which are bad for business.

In other words, Standard American English is no better or worse than any other language or dialect. It is actually a dialect in itself—the dialect by which educated Americans (and, increasingly, people in other parts of the world) communicate in the workplace. That's why it's so important for you to be able to use Standard English effectively. As I noted above, the people you encounter in professional life (not to mention in college!) will judge you, in part, based on how well you use it. Becoming fluent in this dialect is one of the things that will enable you to enter the world of high-paying, professional careers—and succeed and thrive once you get there.

The Five Errors

As I said above, this is not a grammar handbook. I have no desire to delve into the obscurities and intricacies of English grammar here. For that, should you have the need, allow me to recommend John C. Hodges's classic *Harbrace Handbook*, or—if you prefer the online route—Purdue University's Online Writing Lab, known to students as the Purdue OWL. And no, thankfully, you don't have to be a student at Purdue to use that excellent resource.

There are, however, certain grammatical errors that are so common—even among people who ought to know better—that I've decided I need to address them here, in this book on becoming a better writer. Honestly, over the half the people whose e-mails, reports and other professional communications I encounter on a daily basis would be much better writers if they did nothing else but eliminate these five errors.

I'm tempted to add, in describing these errors, that they are also among the most egregious, but I realize that may be a subjective assessment, influenced no doubt by the grammarian in me. (No one who teaches writing manages to suppress that inner demon entirely.) Suffice it to say, these five are certainly among the errors that are most noticeable (at least to people who themselves have a decent grasp of English grammar) and therefore most likely to create, in the reader's mind, a negative impression of the writer. Indeed, it's difficult to encounter these errors consistently, in an individual's writing, and conclude that he or she is fully literate. From there, it's not much of a stretch to begin questioning the writer's intelligence, education, and overall competence. That's probably not accurate, and certainly not fair, but remember: One of your main motivations for learning to write well is so that people will have an overall favorable impression of you.

To do that, you must learn to avoid these five errors. That means, first of all, understanding them and recognizing them when you see them, and second, learning how to fix them, or what to do instead. So, without further adieu, here are the five common writing errors that even the pros make:

Commas Splices and Fused Sentences

One of the overriding rules of standard American English grammar is that you can't combine two sentences with a comma—or without the comma, for that matter. That is, if you have a sentence that grammatically can stand on its own—it has a subject, has a verb, and completes a thought—then it can't be joined (or spliced) onto another stand-alone sentence with just a comma. That's known as a comma splice. Nor can it simply be tacked onto another stand-alone sentence with nothing in between, which is what we call a fused sentence—basically, a comma splice without the comma.

Don't misunderstand: I'm not saying you can't ever combine sentences. Of course you can. In fact, it's often (usually?) a good idea to combine short sentences that contain closely related ideas into longer, more sophisticated sentences. That's one of the marks of good writing. It also just makes sense. Unfortunately, and perhaps ironically, one of the major causes of comma splices is the writer's natural and good desire to combine their ideas into longer sentences. I have no wish to stifle that instinct; indeed, I want to encourage it. What you have to understand, though, is that there are grammatical ways to combine sentences—to combine related ideas—and ungrammatical ways to combine sentences. Comma splices and fused sentences fall into the second category.

Consider the following two short sentences:

I went to the store. Bread was on sale.

Right away, we can see that these two sentences probably belong together. For one thing, they're both very short. And while there's nothing wrong with the occasional short sentence, or maybe even two in a row, it's easy to see that an entire paragraph full of sentences like this would be problematic:

I went to the store. Bread was on sale. I bought some bread. I paid for it at the checkout. I put it in my car. I drove home.

That sounds like a third-grader wrote it. And none of us, in our professional communication, wants to sound a like a third-grader—which is why none of us would ever write something like that. We would naturally try to combine related ideas into longer sentences—and, again, that's a good thing.

Which brings us back to the two sentences we started with. The other reason they obviously ought to be combined, besides the fact that they're short, is that they do indeed contain related thoughts. The exact relationship isn't entirely clear. It could be merely temporal—I was at the store and noticed bread was on sale—or it could be causal: I went to the store because bread was on sale. Either way, simply expressing these ideas as two separate sentences isn't working. We need to combine them.

We can't do that, however, simply by sticking a comma in between them, in place of the period, like so:

I went to the store, bread was on sale.

That's a comma splice. It's the very definition of a comma splice. (And, by the way, if we took out the comma, it would be a fused sentence.) Note, too, that simply putting a comma between those two sentences not only creates a relatively serious grammatical error, it also fails to address the real problem or answer the key question: What do those two ideas have to do with each other? To make that clear, we need words, not just punctuation.

Once we recognize the comma splice for what it is, there are several ways to fix it, grammatically, that also have the happy effect of creating a better, clearer sentence. For instance, we could combine the two sentences using coordination, with a coordinating conjunction (the "FANBOYS" you memorized in elementary school):

I went to the store, and bread was on sale.

or

Bread was on sale, so I went to the store.

Another option is to subordinate one of the two sentences, so it can no longer stand on its own, using a subordinating conjunction:

I went to the store because bread was on sale.

or

When I went to the store, bread was on sale.

Note that in all these examples, the conjunction not only allows us to combine the two sentences grammatically—it also explains the relationship between the two ideas.

Another excellent way to combine related ideas is to use a verbal phrase—essentially, adding "–ing" to the verb. That strategy doesn't always work: "I went to the store, being that bread was on sale" is an ugly sentence on many levels. But when verbal phrases do work, they tend to work very well—and because coordination and subordination are so common, the occasional verbal phrase can make for a nice change of pace, adding more variety to your writing so that all your sentences don't end up sounding the same. Consider the following pair of short, choppy sentences:

I looked back on the day's events. I thought about what had happened.

Here's how that would read if we use a verbal phrase to combine those ideas:

Looking back on the day's events, I thought about what had happened.

Another example:

The eagle spread its wings. It soared over the valley below.

versus

Spreading its wings, the eagle soared over the valley below.

Perhaps you can see for yourself the benefit of using verbal phrases occasionally—how they create flow among your sentences, in addition to adding variety. Admittedly, this probably has more to do with style (which we'll cover in the next chapter) than with grammar, but my point here is that using verbal phrases, like using conjunctions, is a good way to avoid a common grammatical error—the comma splice—while simultaneously writing better sentences. Remember, correctness alone isn't the goal. The goal is good writing.

Sentence Fragments

Another common sentence-level error is the fragment, which is essentially a "sentence" that isn't really a sentence. It can't stand alone, grammatically speaking. Often, a fragment is exactly what the name implies—a piece of a longer sentence that has somehow broken off from the rest, usually because the writer just put the period too soon. For that reason, once you recognize a fragment in your writing, the simplest fix is usually just to attach it to the sentence before or the sentence after, depending on where it fits best.

There are basically three types of sentence fragments:

1. Subordinate clauses, which are "sentences" that begin with a subordinating conjunction. Grammatically, these aren't really sentences at all, because a subordinate (or "dependent") clause, by definition, can't stand alone. It has to be attached to an independent clause, as in the example above: "When I went to the store, bread was on sale." In that sentence, "bread was on sale" is independent, meaning it can stand alone grammatically (which is different from saying that it SHOULD stand alone). "When I went to the store," which begins with the subordinating conjunction "when," is a dependent clause. It can't stand alone.

2. Unattached verbal phrases. Remember that a verbal phrase is not a sentence. It's a phrase. It doesn't have a subject or a verb (a verbal is not a verb). Therefore, it can't stand alone as a sentence. Like a dependent clause, it must be attached to an independent clause. For example, "Spreading its wings," above, is not a sentence. Left by itself on the page, in between two periods, it would

be a fragment. To be grammatically correct, it must be attached to the independent clause, "the eagle soared over the valley below." That creates not just a longer sentence, but a better one.

3. Appositive phrases. An appositive is a word or phrase that further describes a noun, as in "my teacher, Ms. Jones." In that construction, "Ms. Jones" is an appositive to "teacher." Of course, many appositives are much longer, as in this sentence: "After the game, we all went to Chili's, one of my all-time favorite restaurants." The phrase "one of my all-time favorite restaurants" is an appositive to "Chili's." The fact that it's several words long does not change that fact— nor does it make it a sentence. An appositive phrase like "one of my all-time favorite restaurants" cannot stand on its own. By itself, it would be a fragment.

As I suggested above, once you recognize a fragment, the easiest thing to do is just attach it to something else. Usually, that's the best option. But there may be others, depending on the situation, such as eliminating the subordinating conjunction, thereby allowing a formerly dependent clause to stand on its own, or adding an actual verb to a verbal or appositive phrase.

For example, here's a fragment created by an unattached dependent clause:

> **Students should be sure to read their textbook. Because**
> **that's what they'll be tested over.**

The second "sentence" in this example is the one that's not really a sentence. It's a fragment—a dependent clause (beginning with the subordinating conjunction "because") left on its own. Fortunately, there are a couple of easy ways to fix this. We could just attach it to the sentence before, with a comma, or we could rewrite it (perhaps by eliminating the conjunction?) so it can stand alone. For example:

> **Students should be sure to read their textbook, because**
> **that's what they'll be tested over.**

or

> **Students should be sure to read their textbook. That's what**
> **they'll be tested over.**

You can also create a fragment by trying to use a verbal phrase as a separate sentence—something it can't be, because it lacks both a subject and a verb. (Again, a verbAL is not the same as a verb.) Consider these two "sentences":

> **"Fashionistas" are people who consistently wear the latest trends.**
> **Always dressing as if going to a party.**

The first sentence is just fine. It has a subject ("fashionistas") and a verb ("are"). The second sentence, however, presents a problem, because it has neither. "Dressing" is a verbal—a type of modifier—not an actual verb. And even if it were a verb, what would be the subject?

Once again, the error is easily fixed, simply by attaching the fragment to the sentence before:

> **"Fashionistas" are people who consistently wear the latest trends, always dressing as if going to a party.**

Alternatively, we could stay with two separate sentences here, if we wanted to, by adding a subject and verb to the second one:

> **"Fashionistas" are people who consistently wear the latest trends. They're always dressed as if going to a party.**

Note that, in this example, the subject of that second sentence is "they" and the verb is "are." Honestly, I don't know why anyone would choose that option over simply combining the two sentences, but it is grammatically correct (which, as we've noted before, is not the same as "good.")

A final type of fragment occurs when we leave an appositive phrase sitting by itself, rather than being attached to an actual sentence. Just like a verbal phrase, an appositive phrase lacks a subject and verb, so it can't be a sentence:

> **At the end of the semester, you'll submit a "reading journal." A record of your reflections on the course's reading assignments.**

Here we have, in the second "sentence," a noun that could be the subject—"record"— except that it isn't, because there's no verb. And once again, we have the same two options: We can simply tack it onto the sentence before—which is probably where it belongs, since "record" is an appositive to "journal"—or we can add a verb to the second sentence, making it officially an actual sentence:

> **At the end of the semester, you'll submit a "reading journal," a record of your reflections on the course's reading assignments.**

or

> **At the end of the semester, you'll submit a "reading journal." That's a record of your thoughts on the course's reading assignments.**

Note that, in the first example, we could have added "which is" to the second part:

> **At the end of the semester, you'll submit a "reading journal," which is a record of your reflections on the course's reading assignments.**

That wouldn't be wrong; it's just unnecessary. The extra words simply aren't needed in this case, although they might be needed in a different situation. Eliminating unnecessary words—words that don't really accomplish anything—is something we'll talk about more in the next chapter, under the heading of "writing style." I just thought I'd take this opportunity to point out a good example of that principle.

And speaking of writing style, I'd like to say one more thing about fragments before I move on to the next common error. I would be remiss if I failed to acknowledge that writers sometimes use sentence fragments on purpose, for effect. That's fine and often makes for good writing. But I would advise against doing it too much, because too many short dependent clauses or verbal phrases can make your writing sound a bit choppy. Also, let me recommend that you learn and consistently practice the rules for writing strong, grammatical sentences before you start breaking those rules on purpose.

Pronoun Case

One of the most common grammatical errors I see—especially among people who are well educated and therefore, theoretically, ought to know better—has to do with pronoun case. You already know what pronouns are: words that replace nouns. What you might not know (or what you might have known at one point but have since forgotten) is that they come in three main types or cases: subjective, objective, and possessive. It's the first two that sometimes cause problems.

The names are descriptive. In its **subjective** form, a pronoun serves as the **subject** of a sentence, while an **objective** case pronoun is the **object** of a verb or preposition. Below is a chart of common pronouns in their subjective and objective forms:

Subjective	Objective
he	him
she	her
I	me
they	them
we	us
who	whom

Most of us who have been speaking English all our lives understand, usually without even consciously thinking about it, that we use the subjective case when the pronoun is the subject of the sentence. (I've noticed that this is something people who learn English as a second language also master pretty quickly, perhaps because the rule is similar in many other languages.) Hence, we all recognize that the following sentences are grammatically correct:

I went to the store.

He hit the ball.

They were late to the party.

Who is it?

In each of these examples, the highlighted pronoun is the subject of the sentence and thus takes the proper subjective form. We wouldn't dream of saying "Me went to the store" or "Him hit the ball."

Similarly, most of us understand intuitively that we use the objective case when the pronoun is the object of a verb or preposition:

The manager called **her.**

The teacher returned the tests to **them.**

Give it to **me.**

To **whom** is the letter addressed?

Again, this feels natural. We'd never say, "The manager called she" or "Give it to I." Those sound stupid and awkward.

The difficulty arises when we join two pronouns together, particularly in the objective case, and especially when first-person pronouns are involved (I and me). I think that's because we're taught from an early age not to say things like, "My brother and me went to the game." That's bad grammar, because "brother" and "me," in that sentence, form a compound subject, and thus the pronoun, as part of the subject, must be in the subjective case. Correct grammar would be "My brother and I went to the game." As I said, that's drilled into our heads from about first grade on.

Unfortunately, what many seem to hear is that "I" is always correct while "me" is always incorrect, and that's not true. It depends on the case. It's just as wrong to say "He sold his tickets to my brother and I" as it is to say "My brother and me bought them." In the first sentence, both "brother" and "I" are objects of the preposition "to," so the proper case would be the objective: "He sold his tickets to my brother and **me.**" (The second sentence is similar to the example in the paragraph above, so hopefully you can see why it's grammatically incorrect.) Or how about this phrase, which I see and hear all the time: "between you and I." That's incorrect, because "between" is a preposition. It should read, "between you and **me.**"

Whenever you come across passages like those in your own writing, during the editing process, there's a simple way to tell if you've gotten them right: just eliminate the first noun or pronoun in the compound subject. Would you say, "He sold his tickets to I"? Of course not. You'd say, "He sold his tickets to me." The fact that it's a compound—that there's another subject thrown in—doesn't change the grammar. By the same token, you wouldn't say, "Me bought them." You'd say, "I bought them." Again, the compound changes nothing.

Another common pronoun error involves "who" and "whom." Many people can never seem to figure out which one to use. But once you understand that "who" is subjective and "whom" is objective, knowing which one is correct in a given instance becomes relatively easy. When it's the subject of a sentence, you use "who." When it's the object of a verb or preposition, you use "whom."

Admittedly, things can get a little tricky when the sentence is flipped around, as is often the case with "who" and "whom." You just have to read it very carefully to determine if it's a subject or object. Hence, "Whom are you calling?" is correct because "whom," even though it's the first word of the sentence, is not actually the subject. "You" is the subject, with "are" as the verb—essentially, "you are"—even though it's backward here because it's a question. "Whom" is the correct pronoun because it's the object of the verb phrase, "are calling." Again, a good way to check this is to the turn the sentence back around: "You are calling whom?" That makes it a little more obvious. Grammatically, it's the same as saying "You're calling him" instead of "You're calling he."

One last caution about "who" and "whom" before I move on. There are some very common phrases that use "who" even though "whom" is correct. In those cases, it can sound very awkward to use "whom." A few years ago, I wrote an article about networking entitled, "It Really Is Who You Know." I actually used that phrase, or some variation of it, several times in the article. Unfortunately, my editor changed every "who" to "whom," because that's technically correct. "Whom," in that construction, is the object of the verb "know": "You know whom." It just sounds dumb, because we always say, "It's who you know." One reader even wrote, in the comment section, "that's a lot of whoms." I replied, "Yes, it's Old Entish." (If you've never read *The Lord of the Rings*, you probably won't get that joke.)

Misplaced Modifiers

Another common grammatical error involves putting a modifier in the wrong place. Modifiers, as you probably know, are words or phrases that further describe other words or phrases, usually (but not always) nouns. A modifier is often just a single word, like an adjective or adverb, but sometimes it's an entire phrase, like one of those verbal phrases we talked about above. That's where we see the potential for trouble. People rarely put an adjective in front of the wrong noun, but they frequently do so with phrases. The result can be confusing and sometimes even hilarious.

Consider, for example, the following sentences:

> **Rolling down the street, the boy chased the ball.**
> **Wearing only a diaper, the woman ran after her toddler.**
> **Driving off in his car, the dog followed its master.**

Obviously, in all three sentences, the modifying phrases are out of place. It's not "the boy" who's rolling down the street; it's the ball. The woman isn't wearing a diaper; her toddler is. The dog isn't driving a car; its master is. That's easy to see, because these are such egregious and silly examples. Grammatically, though, the reason they don't make sense (and the reason they're funny) is that the noun closest to the modifying phrase isn't actually the word being modified. That violates a basic rule of Standard English grammar, which says that generally speaking a modifier should be right next to whatever it's supposed to be modifying. Or to put it another way, the noun closest to the modifier is the word being modified—whether or not the writer intended it that way.

Again, these are really simple, even simplistic, examples. You might think, "Who would actually write something like that?" Well, you might be surprised. But you're right—I don't often see sentences that silly. What I do see, though, are plenty of sentences like these next two, which at first glance may seem fairly sophisticated but are actually just as nonsensical:

Taking into account the latest sales figures, window displays should be designed to showcase popular trends.

Anticipating the October 31 submission deadline, applications should be completed by the 28th if possible.

What's wrong with those two sentences? The short answer is that both contain misplaced modifiers—just like the examples above, if not as funny. (Both also use the passive voice unnecessarily, but that's something we'll talk about more in the next chapter.) In the first sentence, "taking into account" literally modifies "window displays." But that's ridiculous. Window displays are inanimate objects, incapable of taking anything into account. Only people can do that. Similarly, in the second sentence, "anticipating" literally modifies "applications"—but once again, applications can't anticipate anything. They're just pieces of paper. Written correctly, those sentences would read as follows:

Taking into account the latest sales figures, staff should design window displays to showcase popular trends.

Anticipating the October 31 submission deadline, students should complete their applications by the 28th, if possible.

You see? Staff can actually take sales figures into account, just as students can anticipate a deadline. Those sentences actually make sense.

Okay. Those are made-up examples. Nobody would actually write sentences like that, right? *Au contraire.* Here are a couple of real-life sentences, gleaned just recently from my students' papers (and lightly edited for length and clarity):

Living in Florida, many creatures would make their way into our back yard. Upon arrival, my gaze moved upward from the path I travelled.

Perhaps you can see that the problem here is the same one we identified above. In the first example, although the "creatures" mentioned are indeed "living in

Florida," that's clearly not what the writer meant. She meant that when SHE was living in Florida, all kinds of creatures used to come into her yard. Similar, in the second sentence, it's not "gaze" that "arrived"; the writer is saying that, after he arrived, he looked up. In both cases, the modifiers are misplaced.

And just in case you're thinking to yourself, "Hey, that's no big deal. I understood what those sentences meant to begin with"—well, keep in mind one of the main premises we started with, back in Chapter 1: that clear writing requires clear thinking. Nonsensical sentences, in which (for example) a piece of paper is supposed to anticipate something, are among what writing guru William Zinsser called "the thousand and one adulterants" that weaken our writing, make it difficult for people to follow what we're saying, and (frankly) leave us open to charges of not being very bright. (We'll hear more from Zinsser in the next chapter.)

Remember, there's no such thing as a clear sentence that fundamentally does not make sense. And that's what misplaced modifiers do: create sentences that don't make sense. Learning to avoid them will make your writing better, clearer, stronger, and more intelligent-sounding. Who wouldn't want that?

Subject–Verb Agreement

The last common error I want to talk about in this chapter is one you're probably aware of, because, like pronoun case, it's something that's drilled into our heads from a young age. We all know that, in any sentence, the subject and verb must agree in number. However, as we grow older and gain more education, and our sentences become correspondingly more complex, we find that it's sometime difficult to keep track of exactly which noun is the subject and which subject goes with which verb.

Not to question your intelligence or insult your fifth-grade teacher, but before we go on I'd like to make sure we're all on the same page. When we say that subjects and verbs must agree "in number," we mean that singular subjects require singular verbs while plural subjects require plural verbs. That's elementary. We also know that plural nouns (all subject are nouns) end in –s, while with verbs it's just the opposite: singular verbs end in –s. So, for instance, we wouldn't dream of saying "the boy run." We know it should be either "the boys run" or "the boy runs," depending on how many boys we're talking about. Simple enough.

The problem arises when we start constructing longer sentences with more words in between the subject and the verb—especially if some of those words are other nouns or pronouns, which can look like they might be the subject of the sentence. The most frequent culprit here is the prepositional phrase, because it does end in either a noun or pronoun—but that noun or pronoun is NOT the subject of the sentence. It can't be, because it's the object of the preposition in the phrase, and one of the most fundamental rules of English grammar is that a noun cannot be both a subject and an object at the same time. However, it's easy to confuse the object of a preposition, in a prepositional phrase, with the subject of the sentence, especially if it's closer to the verb than the actual subject. That's a common mistake people make, not because they don't know the difference, but because they're trying to get their thoughts down quickly and not really paying attention—which is fine in a draft but eventually needs to be caught and fixed.

Consider the following sentences:

All the occupants of that overturned car has been taken to the hospital.
Your analysis of this month's sales figures are due 4:00 this afternoon.
A love for animals reveal a sensitive nature.

All three exhibit the same grammatical problem: the subjects and verbs don't agree. In all three cases, the writer has made the verb agree with the nearest noun, which is actually the object of a preposition and not a subject at all. In the first sentence, for example, "car has" would be correct—except that "car" is not the subject. "Car," in that sentence, is the object of the preposition "of": "of that overturned car." The subject is actually "occupants," so the correct verb would be "have": "occupants . . . have." Likewise, the second sentence should read, "Your analysis of this month's sales figures IS due," because the subject of that sentence is singular, "analysis." "Figures" is the object of the preposition "of." And in the third sentence, the subject is "love," not "animals." The correct construction is "A love for animals reveals . . . ."

Once again, these examples are all pretty simplistic, because this is not (as I've stated repeatedly) a grammar handbook. The finer points of English grammar are not within my purview. I just wanted to alert you to some of the more common mistakes that writers make—even writers who should know better, or who DO know better—so that you can take extra care to avoid them. Most educated people know the rules and will be quick to judge those who don't follow them consistently—even if they don't always follow those rules consistently themselves. (You know that old saying about how people who live in glass houses shouldn't throw stones? It should read, "People who live in glass houses shouldn't throw stones—but they always seem to, anyway.")

Let me close this chapter by saying one more thing about grammar, specifically about identifying and fixing your grammatical mistakes: That is a task for the editing phase of the writing process, not for the invention phase or even the drafting phase. In my experience, if you spend too much time in those early stages trying to say things grammatically, the most likely result is that you'll struggle to say anything at all. Better just to let your ideas flow in the invention stage, without any self-editing to build a dam across your stream of consciousness.

Perhaps in a first draft, you can pay a little more attention to grammatical issues, but honestly, I wouldn't advise it. When I'm writing a first draft, I tend just to let things come out however they come out, without worrying if they're correct or not. It's in the last stage, the editing stage—as I move from rough preliminary drafts to more polished later drafts—that I really start paying attention to grammatical issues and fixing them as necessary. At that point, I've already said most of what I was trying to say, so I don't have to worry about stifling my ideas. And of course, I've got to get the document ready for "publication" (whatever that means, depending on the document), so I certainly need to fix whatever needs to be fixed, whether grammatical issues, typos, or otherwise. I just don't worry about those things very much until then.

So by all means, pay attention to your grammar. Fix it as necessary. People will be able to understand you better, and they're less likely to judge you negatively. Just don't worry about "fixing" stuff too early in the process. Wait until you reach the editing stage, then fix away.

DEVELOPING AN ENGAGING STYLE

I ended the last chapter by saying you shouldn't worry too much about fixing grammatical mistakes in the early stages of writing. Instead, save that activity for later drafts as part of the editing process. I'm going to take that idea a step further in this chapter by pointing out that fixing grammatical mistakes is not even the main purpose of editing; its real purpose is to make your writing better. Of course, that might well involve fixing mistakes—if there are errors, you need to correct them—but editing and revising are primarily about writing style, not grammar. To put it another way, it's possible for a piece of writing to be completely free of grammatical errors yet still be difficult to read and understand. That's bad writing, despite any apparent technical proficiency.

So what exactly is writing "style"? That's not an easy question to answer, as style tends to be much more subjective than grammar. Whereas grammar has rules, like the ones we talked about in the last chapter, style is often in the eye of the beholder. As readers, we generally know a good writing style when we see one, but we can't always put our finger on what makes it good. Obviously, it has something to do with clarity, with how easy the writing is to understand, with how much it engages us and makes us want to keep reading. It involves word choice and arrangement, sentence type, length, and variety, and structural factors like paragraph organization and length. None of those elements is "grammatical," strictly speaking, yet all of them contribute to our appreciation of a writer's style—or lack thereof.

But just because style is hard to pin down, that doesn't mean there aren't any guidelines for improving your style. There are, and I intend to talk about several of them in this chapter. Before I do, though, allow me to acknowledge that this has already been done, quite effectively, by people who know more about it than I do. Specifically, I'd like to call your attention to George Orwell's marvelous essay, "Politics and the English Language," in which he was one of the first writers to acknowledge the awkward, stilted, pretentious style that has become so common among educated English speakers. Another essay, "Gobbledygook," by Stuart Chase, from his book *The Power of Words*, builds on Orwell's ideas and offers some hilarious examples of what can happen when writers are more concerned with sounding important that with making themselves understood. And of course, the ultimate and definitive guide to good writing style is William Zinnser's seminal book, *On Writing Well*, which was tremendously influential on me when I was a budding young writer. I will be referencing those works from time to time in this chapter, either directly or indirectly, and I highly recommend that you read them yourself in their entirety.

For the purposes of this book, however, I'm going to do my best to distill the essence of what Orwell, Chase, Zinnser, and others have had to say about good writing. I'll also add my own perspective to the discussion and occasionally cite other top nonfiction writers, such as Malcolm Gladwell. My goal is to help you gain a better sense of what constitutes a good writing style, so that you can begin the long but rewarding journey of improving your own.

Why Does Style Matter?

Again, this is a difficult question. Perhaps the answer is that it doesn't in some contexts. But I would argue that in most contexts, it certainly does.

When I say style doesn't matter much in certain contexts, I'm basically talking about those situations where the writer already has a captive audience, or where the audience has been pre-conditioned to expect bad writing. An example of the former would be a quarterly report that an employee writes for his or her manager. The employee's job is to write it, and the manager's job is to read it. In other words, the manager has a built-in motive to read the report: so that he or she can glean the necessary information in order to make good decisions. The writer doesn't need to "sound good," engage the reader, or make the reader want to keep reading. The reader already has a reason to keep reading.

An example of the second situation—where readers are accustomed to bad writing—would be something like a police report. Even if we haven't read an actual police report ourselves, we've all probably heard passages of a report read aloud over the airwaves, or heard a department spokesperson speak in "official-ese." We know the sentences will be short and stilted, that the report will be heavily jargon-laden, and that it will almost certainly leave some of our questions unanswered. We expect the writing to be bad, because we've heard such reports before. And it is. Bad, I mean.

In both those examples, however, I would argue that we can accept a degree of bad writing, but beyond that, we still have certain expectations. The writing can be dull and boring, for instance—who realistically expects better?—but it should at least be clear. Even if those sentences are stilted, at least they should contain the required information, phrased so that we can access it. That's a minimum expectation. So in that sense, writing style matters at least a little bit, even in those situations.

I would also argue, though, that even in the driest, most mundane and bureaucratic situations imaginable (like the ones cited above), good writing is still a virtue. No, the employee writing for his boss doesn't necessarily have an obligation to engage her—but it would certainly be better for her, and for him, if she were engaged. She's probably somewhat more likely to absorb and remember what she reads, and less likely to want to poke out her own eyes, if the writing actually presents the material in an interesting and compelling manner. Think of it this way: If you were the boss, and you were constantly reading through incredibly dry and boring reports, and then you came across one that wasn't dry and boring, how would you react? What would you think about that employee?

Likewise, no one really expects a police officer to be a good writer. Being clear is enough. But what if a given officer (or nurse, or teacher, or whatever) actually is a pretty good writer? What do you think that might do for his or her career?

The truth, as I noted back in Chapter 5, is that virtually everyone who gets a college degree and goes into professional life is going to be a writer, regardless of their field, whether they want to or not. And the higher up they climb on the corporate ladder, the more writing they're going to have to do. But the corollary to that truism is that the people who do it best—the best communicators—are the ones who are most likely to climb the ladder the highest and the fastest. That's where good writing comes in, and that's why it's important for you to work at developing your writing style, whether you plan to be a "professional writer" or not.

One more thing about style before I move on. When I talk about writing style, I'm not talking about using a lot of big words and long sentences to make yourself sound smarter without actually saying anything. Quite the opposite, in fact. Nor am I talking about flowery, poetic language, designed to make people marvel at what a great writer you are. I believe that, too, is usually counterproductive.

No, I've always believed that the best writing style is one that is essentially invisible—readers don't notice it, one way or the other. All they notice are the ideas the writer is attempting to convey, and they are carried along by the prose without even realizing they're being carried along. Just like bad writing can be off-putting because it bores the reader and sometimes obscures the meaning, so too can "good" writing be off-putting, if it's ostentatiously good. When I read something that's poorly written, I usually find myself focusing on the writing itself, not on what the writer is trying to say. But the same is true of very good writing, in the literary sense. Whenever I find myself noticing how beautifully written a piece is, I realize that I'm not actually paying attention to what it says.

That's why I say a good writing style is invisible. You want readers to pay attention to what you say, not how you say it. You want them to be engaged without even knowing they're engaged.

What Is a Bad Writing?

A couple of chapters ago, I talked about what constitutes "good writing," in my view. It's only fair that I give equal time to its opposite.

As I suggested above, "bad writing" doesn't just involve poor grammar. That's a separate issue, which we addressed in the last chapter. It's quite possible for a piece of writing to contain several grammatical errors and yet still be basically readable, still get its point across. The bad grammar might be an obstacle for some readers, and it certainly won't present the writer (or their ideas) in the best possible light. But that doesn't necessarily make the writing awful.

Conversely, it is entirely possible—even likely, in certain scenarios—for a piece of writing to be completely devoid of grammatical errors and yet at the same time be truly awful—boring, tedious, virtually unintelligible. Because even though "ungrammatical" may, to a certain extent, equal "bad," "grammatical" does not therefore equal good (as we've all been led to believe since first grade). Grammatical is merely a starting point, a baseline. There are usually a number of different ways to say the same thing that are all equally grammatical. (There will be some that are ungrammatical, too, as we saw in the last chapter.) A good writer starts with grammatical constructions and from those, chooses the one that most clearly conveys the point, engages the reader, sounds the best, and fits most smoothly with the other sentences around it. That's what we mean when we talk about a good "style." It goes way beyond grammar.

A bad writing style, then, is one that is not readable. It fails to engage the reader and may well be difficult to understand—not because the reader doesn't know the definitions of the individual words, but because the way they're put together either doesn't seem to make sense or else actively obscures the meaning of the sentence as a whole. Bad writing is unnecessarily verbose (that means long-winded), using long words when shorter ones would have worked just fine. One example that Orwell provides, in "Politics and the English Language," involves a well-known passage from the Old Testament book of Ecclesiastes:

> I returned and saw under the sun, that the race is not to the swift, nor the battle to the strong, neither yet bread to the wise, nor yet riches to men of understanding, nor yet favour to men of skill; but time and chance happeneth to them all.

Orwell then renders this beautifully clear passage in modern English:

> Objective considerations of contemporary phenomena compel the conclusion that success or failure in competitive activities exhibits no tendency to be commensurate with innate capacity, but that a considerable element of the unpredictable must invariably be taken into account.

Do you see the point Orwell is trying to make? The writing in that second passage may be technically correct: flawless grammar, multiple polysyllabic words that mean exactly what the writer intends. But, taken as a whole, it's all but unreadable. Readers certainly do not take from that passage the kind of clear meaning they draw from the first one. It's as if the writer is trying to show off all the big words and impressive-sounding phrases he knows, rather than actually trying to communicate ideas. It's not good writing because no one, given the choice, would want to read it—and if they did, they probably wouldn't understand it, anyway.

There's another dynamic worth noting here, too: The writer of that second example is not someone who is stupid or poorly educated. Quite the opposite, in fact. Look at all the big words he knows! (And I'd bet anything it is a "he.") Look at the perfect grammar! Most of the bad writing that we encounter, in our college career and our professional lives, does not come from people who don't know better. That would be much easier to accept. Unfortunately, the tendency toward this kind of bad writing tends to increase with an individual's level of education. You would think that the more educated people are, the better they would write. Sadly, the opposite seems to be true.

The explanation for this dynamic is that bad writing tends to perpetuate itself. Students read textbooks and scholarly articles that are poorly written—for reasons we'll get into in a bit—then listen to professors who pontificate in their overblown, "scholarly" language, and conclude that that's how smart people must talk and write. To appear smart themselves—because they are smart—they seek to emulate those models. Then they get into the workforce, where it seems like the people who succeed are the ones who sound impressive, whether they're actually saying anything or not. So they learn to sound like they're saying important stuff without worrying about whether it's truly important. Their goal is for readers and listeners to shake their heads and marvel at how smart they are—not to actually convey a set of ideas.

That is bad writing. That is where bad writing comes from. The purpose of writing (or speaking) in a professional setting is to convey ideas, to inform and ultimately persuade, as we will see in subsequent chapters. It's not about demonstrating how smart you are. Trust me: If you are genuinely smart, and if you're able to communicate your ideas in ways that engage people and that they can understand, they won't have any problem ultimately acknowledging your brilliance.

The Characteristics of a Good Writing Style

There's plenty we could say about what constitutes a good writing style. Heck, we could write a whole book about it. Then again, William Zinsser already did that, and I only have one chapter to devote to the topic. So I'm going to spend my time talking about what I believe are the three most important characteristics of good writing: It's clear, it's concise, and it's conversational.

Good writing is clear. Perhaps this sounds like one of those "duh" statements. Of course good writing is clear; isn't that kind of the definition of good writing? Well, yes. Unfortunately, recognizing that this is true and actually doing it appear to be two different things. To put it another way, however obvious it may seem that written communication should be clear, it is no small matter to be able to express oneself clearly in writing. My experience suggests that the majority of writers—and I'm talking here about college-educated people—can't do it. Or maybe it would be more accurate to say that they don't do it, because I'm convinced they could, if they really wanted to. The problem is, they don't care. They don't think it's important.

I would argue that clear writing is vitally important. Think about how much our culture, our technology, our politics depend on the clear transmission of information. There are things people simply have to know in order to function on a daily basis—to drive a car, to prepare their food, to do their jobs, to use their devices, to pay their taxes, to vote. In our society, the majority of that information is communicated through writing—mostly, these days, on a screen, but that is still writing, nonetheless. (As an aside, note that advances in technology have not made writing less common as a form of communication; if anything, they've made it more common.)

The essence of the problem, as I observed above, is that the more education people acquire, the more trouble they seem to have expressing themselves in plain language, so that others (including those with less education) can understand them. Perhaps that's because their main goal is not for people to understand them—it's for people to be impressed by how smart they are. So they litter their sentences with big words (that don't always mean exactly what they think they mean), qualifiers, and inflated constructions—like saying "give consideration to" rather than just saying "consider." Phrases like that make a piece of writing longer—which some consider a virtue in its own right—and give it more apparent heft, but they don't do anything to make the ideas more accessible. If anything, taken together, they do just the opposite.

One of the keys to clear writing, then, is conciseness, which I'm going to cover separately in my next subsection. But another key involves choosing exactly the right words, words that express your ideas as simply and straightforwardly as possible. Too many writers look at a word like "give" or "use" and conclude that it's too short; there must be a longer word that looks and sounds more impressive. So they substitute "convey" or "utilize." But those words aren't always better just because they're longer. Longer, Latinate words, due to the nature of Latin, tend to express subtler nuances of meaning. Sometimes they're preferable because they're more precise. But other times, the short word works just fine. In that case, for the sake of clarity, use it.

But how do you know when to use the longer word and when to use the shorter one? Here's a good rule of thumb: Use the longer word when it's the only word that carries the desired meaning—like "phenomenon"—or when it replaces an entire phrase. "Procrastinate" is a good word because it means "to put something off"—four words, the meaning of which I can easily express in one. The same with "compensate" (to make up for) and "vacillate" (to go back and forth). But there's no reason to say "masticate" when you mean "chew," "expectorate" when you mean "spit," or "prevaricate" when you mean "lie." That's just showing off—and it does nothing either to engage the reader or to enable comprehension. Again, quite the opposite.

None of this is means that you shouldn't work to acquire a large vocabulary. You certainly should. Having a large vocabulary is one of the hallmarks of a well-educated person, and it enables you to express those subtle shades of meaning that we mentioned above. Because sometimes you DO need "prevaricate," which doesn't always mean exactly the same thing as "lie," although they're very close. The former carries nuance not found in the latter, and there will be times when such nuance is important. My point is simply this: If you mean "lie," then just say "lie." Don't toss in a hundred-dollar word solely to prove how smart you are. Occasionally, that hundred-dollar word won't mean exactly what you think it means (Zinsser cites the example of "sanguine" versus "sanguinary"—look them up), and then you're likely to be embarrassed when it turns out that some readers know the difference. The trick, again, is to be as precise as possible, using exactly the right word at exactly the right time. Not that anyone every fully achieves that, but it's the goal.

Besides using words that don't mean what we think they mean (hat tip: Inigo Montoya), we also have a tendency to use filler words that don't necessarily mean anything in particular—like the word "thing" for instance. I'm as bad about this as anybody, substituting "thing" whenever I can't think of what something is actually called. (See, I just did it.) Sometimes, I don't even bother to think about what it might be called; I just say "thing" and move on.

In a rough draft, that's fine. It keeps me moving forward, instead of constantly stopping and second-guessing myself, which only serves to slow my momentum. But when I'm editing, I always stop at imprecise words like "thing" and ask myself, "what thing? What exactly am I attempting to identify here?" Sometimes, the answer is that I'm not sure, in which case I need to give it a little more thought. If I don't know what I'm talking about, how can I expect the reader to know what I'm talking about? Other times, there isn't really a word for what I'm trying to describe, so "thing" is the best I can do. But at least half the time, and maybe two-thirds of the time, I can find a better, more descriptive noun than "thing."

Again, we all do this, using fillers instead of meaningful words. As I said, I'm as bad about it as anybody. The problem is, most people don't even recognize that they do it, and if they do recognize it, they make no attempt to do better. That's why one of the qualities that characterizes bad writing bad is that it's sloppy—rambling, repetitive, and imprecise. Note that my first draft of that sentence read "One of the things that makes writing bad is that it's sloppy." In my editing, I realized I could do better than "thing"; what I really meant was "quality," so I substituted that word. I also decided that "characterize," in this context, is a more precise word than "make." That's a quick little mini-lesson in editing that also illustrates what I mean by working to become more precise.

The last bad habit that leads to lack of clarity is overusing the passive voice. The natural order of a sentence, as I noted back in Chapter 7, is subject–verb–object. That way, the reader always knows who is doing what to whom or what. Of course, the sentence may include a lot more information than that, in the form of prepositional phrases, modifiers, and so forth. But the basic structure of the sentence makes it very clear what's happening.

The passive voice perverts that structure, using the natural object of the verb as the subject. It essentially turns the sentence around backwards. Consider these two simple sentences:

He hit the ball.
The ball was hit.

The first is in active voice. We know who performed the action, we know what action he performed, and we know what object the action was performed upon. In the second sentence, however, that object—the ball—is technically the subject of the sentence. That's an example of the passive voice—when the true subject of the sentence, the person or thing the writer is talking about, isn't actually performing the action. In fact, that second sentence doesn't even tell us who performed the action; to convey that information, the writer would need to add two words—"by him"—which would violate the principle of conciseness by using six words to express an idea that can be plainly stated in four.

Obviously, this is a pretty Mickey-Mouse example. Both sentences, in this case, are perfectly clear. The passive voice, in the second sentence, doesn't really affect our understanding of what's going on. But consider longer sentences like these:

Knowing how to use Microsoft Word and Excel spreadsheets is also expected.
Mileage must be logged when a company car is driven.

I would suggest that both sentences are somewhat difficult to understand, even though neither is particularly egregious. Let's just say that they're a lot less clear than they could be, largely because of the unnecessary use of the passive voice.

A bigger problem with both sentences, however, is that they leave much unstated. Who needs to know how to use Word and Excel? Who expects it of them? Who must log their mileage? Who is driving the car? The answers to those questions, given the construction of the sentences, can only be inferred by the reader. We assume that job candidates need to be able to use those software programs, and that the prospective employer expects them to. We assume that employees must log their miles when they use a company car. And such assumptions are probably correct, in this instance. But will they always be? And should writers leave such important points to the imagination of the reader? Why don't we just say what we mean:

We expect candidates to be proficient in Microsoft Word and Excel spreadsheets.
Employees must log their miles when using a company car.

A couple more points about passive voice before I move on. First, I'm not saying that it's always bad. There are times when it's the best alternative. For instance, I've used it twice in the sentences above: "what object that action was performed upon" and "can only be inferred by the reader." In both cases, in the editing stage, I toyed with different ways of writing the sentence—but I couldn't come up with anything that sounded better, made the point any clearer, or flowed as well with the rest of the sentence and the other sentences around it. (Can you? Give it a try.) Sometimes the passive voice works just fine. And sometimes you're just stuck with it, for lack of a better alternative. But once again, as an editor, you should always stop when you notice that you've used the passive voice and see if you can improve the sentence by converting it to active. Most of the time, you can.

Finally, it's only fair to note that sometimes professional communicators— that is, professional arguers—use the passive voice intentionally in order to achieve exactly what we talked about above: obscuring their meaning. Hence, the politician says, "Mistakes were made" because he or she wouldn't dream of saying, "So-and-so made a mistake," much less, "I made a mistake." That would assign too much responsibility and invite blame. Or the chair of a large committee writes a report that concludes, "The committee is of the opinion that changes need to be made to the current curriculum." No way they're going to come right out and say, "We think the English Department needs to change its curriculum." There's too much political liability inherent in a statement like that.

So if your goal is to be unclear, then, hey, the passive voice is an excellent tool. But if you actually want to be understood, it should be avoided most of the time. Excuse me, I meant to say, you should avoid it most of the time.

Good writing is concise. I mentioned conciseness briefly above because it is inextricably linked to clarity. It has to do with choosing exactly the right word or set of words to express your idea, but it also has to do with not using too many words, especially where they're unnecessary. As I like to tell my students, never use two words where one will do—or ten words where eight will do. Or twenty where twelve will do. (You get the idea.) Orwell, in "Politics and the English Language," puts it this way, as one of his six rules for good writing: "If it is possible to cut a word out, always cut it out."

Note that the point is not to create simplistic sentences that sound like a first-grader wrote them. (Like the books I used learning to read, way back in kindergarten: "See Spot run. Look, Jane. Spot runs.") As you progress in your education, and in your professional life, you will naturally be dealing with increasingly complex ideas. Expressing those ideas in writing will often require complex language and sentences. That's why it's important, as I noted above, to develop a well-stocked vocabulary. The point is not to use any more words than you have to. If it takes twenty-five words to express an idea in a sentence, then by all means—use twenty-five words. But if you can do it in fewer, then do it in fewer. Writing a longer sentence than necessary is just another form of showing off, without any benefit to the reader. If anything, the reader is less likely to understand you, the more words you use—and especially, the more unnecessary words you use.

The problem is that we tend to assume otherwise, because of the models we've been exposed to throughout our education. We grow up believing that smart people use lots of words, and so, wanting to appear smart, we learn to use lots of words—lots more than we need, sometimes. As Zinsser puts it in *On Writing Well*, "Our national tendency is to inflate and thereby sound important." (I'm sure it's not just our nation that does this.)

In fact, though, just the opposite is true. Inflating our sentences doesn't really make us seem more important, intelligent, or knowledgeable. Well, maybe it will for a time, but eventually people will see through us—they'll come to realize that the emperor has no clothes. Eventually, we just start to sound pompous, even silly. To put it another way, it doesn't require a lot of intelligence to take a fairly simple idea—like "children learn to do things by watching"—and make it sound more complicated than it is: "Experience has shown that, in the psychomotor domain, as opposed to the affective domain, children can generally be classified as profoundly visual learners." No, true genius lies in taking complex ideas (or ideas that appear complex) and putting them in terms regular people can understand—translating the second sentence into the first one, rather than vice-versa.

Zinsser calls this tendency to litter our sentences with unnecessary (and often meaningless) words "clutter," which he identifies as the "disease of American writing." (Again, I doubt this disease is confined to America.) "We are," he says, "a society strangling in unnecessary words, circular constructions, pompous frills, and meaningless jargon." The way to combat clutter, he argues—what he calls "the secret to good writing"—is

> to strip every sentence to its cleanest components. Every word that serves no function, every long word that could be a short word, every adverb that carries the same meaning that is already in the verb, every passive construction that leaves the reader unsure of who is doing what—these are the thousand and one adulterants that weaken the strength of a sentence.

Stripping every sentence to its cleanest components is undoubtedly good advice. But how do we do it? Zinsser offers some advice, in the sentence quoted above and elsewhere in his book, as does Orwell. Once again, I recommend that you read them both. But for the purposes of this chapter, and in the interests of brevity, let me just offer a few concrete tips to start you down the road to stronger, cleaner, more concise sentences.

First, pay attention to the advice I've already given about not using a long word when a short one will do and not using two words where one will suffice. Note that both Zinsser and Orwell echo those sentiments. (Well, to be precise, I'm actually echoing them, not the other way around, but whatever—we're all saying the same things.) They also reinforce my suggestion to avoid the passive voice whenever possible, on the grounds that it both clouds the meaning of your sentences AND requires more words. Those are good places to start.

Second, as you edit, be on the lookout for words that aren't necessary in context. These can often be short, common words, like "of" and "that." Is there any practical difference between "all of my friends" and "all my friends"? Or between "the movie that we saw" and "the movie we saw"? In both cases, the answer is "no." There's no difference. That means, in the first example, we don't need the word "of" and in the second, we don't need "that." Which is not to say that you never need "of" or "that." Sometimes you do. They're perfectly good words that often express exactly what you're trying to say. But sometimes they don't. Sometimes they're just extra, superfluous, dropped into the sentence because we're used to using them—or because we think it makes the sentence sound more "proper." (It doesn't.) Remember: Words are like employees. If they're not doing anything, get rid of them.

Third, note what Zinsser said about adverbs. Too often we use adverbs that are already implied by the verb, like "smiled happily." Really? Sure, it's possible to smile another way—to smile ruefully, for instance—but in the absence of any other descriptor, smiling is itself an indication of happiness. We probably don't need "happily" in that sentence. For that matter, we can often apply the same rule to adjectives. Do we really need that long string of adjectives in front of that noun? Really? All three of them? Can't we get by with just one? Usually, the answer is "yes."

And finally, building off that last point—and going back to what I said earlier—the key to creating strong, concise sentences is to put some thought into your verbs and nouns. Instead of saying "the fire burned brightly in the hearth," I can just say "the fire blazed in the hearth." That eliminates an unnecessary adverb. Similarly, rather than describing my "old, rustic, log house," I can simply tell you about my "cabin." That one noun eliminates all three of those adjectives.

Learning to strip your sentences clean will take some time. As you can probably tell from certain passages in this book, I'm still working at it. But that doesn't mean it's not good advice. It is. I'm trying to follow it, and you should, too. The key is to admit that clutter is a problem—kind of like an alcoholic acknowledging their addiction. When it comes to writing, many of us are wordoholics. Once we recognize the problem, we can start working to correct it, working to eliminate unnecessary words and make our sentences as clean, clear, and concise as we possibly can.

One last point about conciseness before we move on: Sometimes, being *precise*, as we discussed above, is more important than being *concise*. Sometimes, in order to say what you mean, you have to use more words, not fewer—which may, in some cases, require you to *add* words when you're editing instead of taking them out.

For example, I was editing an institutional document recently that read, "Qualified students who wish to do so may transition seamlessly to the main campus or to another university." Unfortunately, that isn't quite accurate. Students on the branch campus where I work can indeed transition seamlessly to the main campus—but they cannot transition seamlessly to another university. They have to transfer, just like any other students, and the transfer process is hardly seamless. As anyone who has ever transferred from on institution to another knows, there are seams. Accordingly, I rewrote that sentence to read as follows: "Qualified students who wish to do so may transition seamlessly to the main campus or transfer to another university." In order for that sentence to make sense—to be precise in its meaning—I actually had to add two words.

Good writing is conversational. So far in this chapter, I've mostly just been agreeing with the acknowledged experts, people like Orwell and Zinsser. In fact, I pretty much borrowed all that advice about clarity and conciseness from them (although, since I cited them, I can't be accused of plagiarism). Basically, they said it about as well as it can be said long before I showed up. I've just been trying to summarize their main points, because I believe those are things you need to know.

Here, though, is where I'm going to go out on a limb a little bit and talk about one of my own pet peeves—conversational writing. Not that I think Orwell or Zinsser would disagree, although since they're dead, you'll have to take my word for that. I actually think most professional writers would agree with me—but a lot of writing teachers, along with other teachers and professors, might not. I just think they're wrong, for reasons I'll explain in the following paragraphs.

Essentially, the question is whether we should teach people, in high school or college or beyond, to write in an academic style or in a more conversational style. I would argue for the latter, since most people (thank goodness) don't go on to become academics. Instead, they do other things with their lives—and isn't college supposed to prepare people for life?

This discussion is actually part of a much larger debate over what constitutes good writing. As I always tell my first-year composition students, when I'm trying to correct all the misconceptions about writing they've picked up in high school— you can't use personal pronouns or start a sentence with a conjunction, etc.—the only reasonable standard for good writing is what good writers actually do. How many of our best nonfiction writers, the ones who are widely read and have a genuine impact, write in an academic style? Virtually none.

More to the point, how many professionals these days, apart from actual academics, write in an academic style? Again, almost none. Of course, lawyers and businesspeople have their own stylistic quirks, which can be even more annoying than academic prose. But the very best writers, in practically every field, avoid those quirks. They write in a conversational style.

Admittedly, there are conversations and there are conversations. Two academics talking to each other would sound very different from two corporate types, who would sound different from two restaurant managers or two custodians. Likewise, a college professor writing for students would sound different from a professor writing for other professors—or at least, that's how it should be, although many textbook writers seem to forget it (speaking of clarity and conciseness).

What distinguishes a conversational style is not just that it's less formal (although it usually is) or that it avoids stuffy, made-up "rules" like the ones just mentioned (although it usually does), but that it attempts to approximate an actual conversation between a writer and a reader. In order to do that, the writer must first recognize that a reader exists, which academics often fail to do. Most scholarly writing (at least in the humanities) sounds to me like the writer is having a conversation with himself or herself. Perhaps that's consistent with the introspective, philosophical nature of the academic enterprise—let's not forget what the "Ph." in "Ph.D." stands for—but it doesn't translate well to the world outside of academia, which all but a handful of people inhabit.

Consider, for example, the following passage, which I chose more or less at random after surfing my college's online journal collection. (I'm not going to say where I got it, exactly, because my objective is not to criticize or embarrass anyone.)

> Last and highest on the thinking continuum is the evaluative type question that is considered a staple of published literature-based reading series. Usually found at the end of a story, this type of question requires student learners to go over their own opinions or evaluations. . . . Some examples of evaluative questions for teaching literature include, How are you similar to the character? What is your opinion of the character or events in the story? Why do you think the author wrote the story? . . . Bos and Vaughn (2002) similarly noted categories that help student learners distinguish between literal and interpretive questions—skills that they titled textually explicit, textually implicit, and scripturally implicit.

I say that I chose this passage "more or less at random" because I was looking specifically for something that would serve as a classic example of academic prose without being too egregious—which this isn't. It has all the earmarks of traditional scholarly writing: long, clunky sentences, passive voice, and recurrent jargon. Yet the meaning itself is fairly easy to grasp, and I think most of us understand why it's written the way it is. As academic writing goes, this is better than some and no worse than most.

What this passage isn't, however, is engaging. I don't know about you, but the writer lost me midway through the first sentence. Speaking for a moment as a human being, and not as an academic, I would read something like this only if I absolutely had to, and then I wouldn't be too happy about it. Ask yourself one simple question: After slogging through that short excerpt, do you have any desire to read the rest of the essay?

Me neither.

So why isn't the passage engaging? Because the author doesn't even try. He or she makes (or, more likely, they make) no attempt to engage a real live person who might be reading. It's almost as if that person, the reader, doesn't exist—as if the subject matter is so ponderously significant that it transcends any human interaction. That attitude, I've observed, is characteristic of academic prose, where the emphasis is typically on the ideas themselves rather than on communicating them effectively. You can either get it or not, the writer seems to be saying, and if you don't, that's your problem.

Now compare the previous passage to the following, from Malcolm Gladwell's bestselling book *Outliers*:

> The "achievement gap" is a phenomenon that has been observed over and over again, and it typically provokes one of two responses. The first response is that disadvantaged kids simply don't have the same ability to learn as children from more privileged backgrounds. They're not as smart. The second, slightly more optimistic conclusion is that, in some ways, our schools are failing poor children: we simply aren't doing a good enough job of teaching them the skills they need. But here's where Alexander's study gets interesting, because it turns out neither of those explanations rings true.

Now do you want to read more? Why? Because the writer has engaged you. And how did he do that? By varying sentence length to create a subtle sense of pace. By smoothing out the rough edges of the sentences through liberal use of contractions (generally considered a no–no in academic prose). By not only addressing the readers directly but including us in the discussion ("our schools," "we . . . aren't"). Using simple, everyday words when such words carry the desired meaning, while not altogether avoiding longer words (like "phenomenon") when needed. "Simple," in this case, does not mean "simplistic."

Granted, Gladwell is one of the very best writers working today. But isn't that exactly what we ought to be teaching our students—what the best writers do? I've never bought the argument that professional writers have some sort of license the rest of us don't. That's like saying Steph Curry can execute a crossover dribble because he's Steph Curry, while the rest of us have to play like extras in a 1950 phys-ed film. I say if you can crossover dribble, go for it. And if you can't, work on it until you can.

Even that analogy doesn't really illustrate my point, though, because what Gladwell does isn't fancier or more difficult. Granted, it's not easy to write as gracefully as he does, although he certainly makes it look that way. But the sort of conversational style he uses is, if anything, more natural and intuitive than what we spend years teaching students in high school and college. Perhaps the main reason students struggle to write conversationally is they've been told since kindergarten that it's not acceptable—even though it's perfectly appropriate for the vast majority of the writing they'll be doing throughout their lives.

I, for one, am here to tell you that you can write conversationally, and you should. Because—speaking again as a human being, and as a reader—whether I'm perusing a scholarly tome or checking out the latest credit card offer in the mail, I'd much rather encounter a Gladwell wannabe than some pseudo-academic poser.

A Few Words on Paragraphing

We've talked a lot in this chapter so far about language and sentences. Now I'd like to address the issue of paragraphing. Because the way you construct your paragraphs has a lot to do with the reader's ability to follow and understand what you're saying.

The main rule, when it comes to paragraphing, is that you should do it. That is, you should break up a longer piece of writing into shorter segments, which we call paragraphs. These segments serve two purposes. First of all, they are organizational units, a way of bringing related ideas together in one place so readers can see that they're related and better understand how they're related and what that has to do with your larger point. For that reason, paragraphs often begin with a topic sentence, which expresses the main idea of that paragraph, and the sentences that follow all either expand on that topic sentence or explain the sentence immediately before. When you get to a point in your writing where that's no longer true—where you're ready to move on to a different topic—it's time to start a new paragraph. Most of you probably understood what I just said, because it's what we're all taught about paragraphing in school.

However, paragraphs also serve another function, one we rarely talk about: They are VISUAL units, helping to break the longer piece of writing into more manageable pieces. Research has shown that the way a document appears on the page has a significant impact on the reader, completely separate from what it actually says. As readers, when we see a long, unbroken section of print, we tend to have an adverse reaction. We assume it will be tedious, boring, dense, and difficult to read—which might well turn out not to be true, once we read it. It might be an intensely interesting explanation or a fun story. We don't know. All we see is a really long passage and think to ourselves, "bore-ring." That's one of the reasons we try to break our writing into paragraphs—to make it "bite-size" for the reader.

The question, then, is "how long should a paragraph be?" Over the years, most of us have heard the standard answers. A paragraph should be at least five sentences long. A paragraph should be between 75 and 125 words. And so forth. It's not that those guidelines (which are not, by the way, actual rules) are wrong; it's just that they're inadequate. They don't take into account the type of writing, the size of the font, or the type of document.

So I'm going to give you a rule of thumb that I believe works well in most writing situations: the "four-inch rule." That is, in academic and professional documents, your paragraphs should average between four and five inches in length. Note that we're talking about an average. It certainly doesn't mean every single paragraph should be exactly 4.5 inches long. Stylistically speaking, variety is just as important in paragraph length as it is in sentence length. If we say that the average sentence, for college-educated professionals, is about eighteen words, that doesn't mean every sentence is exactly sentence eighteen words. It means there will be some five-word sentences and some twenty-five-word sentences, but mostly they'll be between fifteen and twenty words. The same is true of paragraphs. You might have the occasional two-inch paragraph and the (hopefully) rare ten-inch paragraph, but most are somewhere between three and six inches.

In other words, when you see that you have a couple of short paragraphs (three inches or less) back-to-back, you should seriously think about combining them, if you can. If it makes sense. Maybe you can't, logically, because the topics are completely different. But maybe you can. By the same token, when you notice that you've written a really long paragraph, eight inches or more, you should consider breaking it into two paragraphs, if you can find a logical place to break it. Again, maybe you can't. But I think you'd be surprised at how often you can break a long paragraph and find that the writing still flows just fine and makes perfect sense. You might need to edit a little, changing the wording at the end of one paragraph and/or at the beginning of the next in order to create a smooth transition—but then again, you might be surprised at how often you don't have to change a single word.

And by the way, I believe the second function of the paragraph actually trumps the first one. Even if all the ideas in a paragraph are related to each other, and the paragraph therefore holds together logically, if there are simply so many related ideas that the paragraph ends up being ten or twelve inches long, you need to break it. Nobody wants to read a twelve-inch paragraph.

Using Transitions

The last topic I'd like to cover in this chapter, under the heading of writing style, is using transitions. These are words and phrases that enable the reader to move smoothly from one idea to the next, from one sentence or paragraph to the next. They also demonstrate the logical connection between ideas and sentences. Is this new idea because of the last one? Instead of? In addition to? Transitions answer those questions and more. Indeed, we could say that effective use of transitions is key to a good writing style, if we define a good style as one that engages readers and allows them to easily understand what the writer is saying.

There's no way I could list all the possible words and phrases that writers typically use to form transitions, even if I could think of them all (which I probably can't). But here's a short list of some common transitions, as examples of what I'm talking about:

however	because	in addition	conversely
therefore	moreover	also	another
instead	indeed	on the other hand	first, second, third
also	thus	by the same token	besides

Usually those words or phrases appear at the beginning of a sentence, like so:

We've had record-breaking cold for the past week. However, the updated forecast suggests that a warming trend is on its way.

But sometimes it sounds better to put the transition a little later in the sentence:

We've had record-breaking cold for the past week. The updated forecast, however, suggests that a warming trend is on its way.

Let me close this section by acknowledging, in all fairness, that some writers (like me) have a tendency to overuse transitions. Sometimes transitions, as useful as they are, can fall into the category Zinsser calls "adulterants," weakening rather than improving sentences because they aren't really needed. Sometimes the transition is contained in the meaning of the sentence. Sometimes it's implicit in the sequence of sentences. When I'm writing a first draft, I don't worry too much about over-using transitions (just like I don't worry too much about a lot of things, in a first draft). But later, when I'm editing, I always look very carefully at my transitions to see if they're necessary, and I get rid of the ones that aren't.

That's ultimately what a good writing style is all about: saying everything that needs to be said without saying anything that doesn't need to be said. No one can achieve that ideal consistently, but it's always what we're shooting for.

REFERENCES

Chase, Stuart. *The Power of Words*. New York: Harcourt, 1954.

Gladwell, Malcolm. *Outliers*. New York: Little, Brown, 2008.

Jenkins, Rob. "The Case for Conversational Writing." *chroniclevitae.com*. *The Chronicle of Higher Education*. 14 August 2014.

Orwell, George. "Politics and the English Language." *Horizon*, April 1946:252-265.

Zinsser, William. *On Writing Well*. New York: Harper Collins, 1976.

MAKING (AND WINNING) ARGUMENTS

As the title suggests, this book is about thinking and writing. Accordingly, Chapters 1 through 4 were about thinking, while Chapters 4 through 8 were about writing. In the next two chapters, I want to tie all those concepts together by examining ways to USE your thinking skills IN your writing. Then we'll close out the book by looking at a couple of special writing situations.

Specifically, in this chapter, I'd like to talk about using your thinking skills to make arguments—because that's something you're going to be doing for the rest of your life. In school, you make plenty of academic arguments (we usually call them "term papers"), for the (supposed) purpose of learning how to do it—make arguments, that is. And then, when you get out of school and move into the workforce, you go right on making arguments, except for real: trying to persuade people to review your application, call you in for an interview, hire you, buy your product or service, provide you with resources, adopt your proposal, follow your directions—the list goes on. Some of those arguments will be made in person, either one-on-one or to larger groups, but the majority will take the form of written documents: letters, reports, proposals, etc. That has always been true, but it's more true today than ever because of e-mail and social media.

It follows, then, that one of the most important skills you can develop, professionally speaking, is the ability to make effective arguments in writing—essentially, as I said back in Chapter 5, to get people to do what you want them to do. That's what this chapter is about; indeed, it's what the entire book is about. Now I'm just going to be really explicit about it.

Argumentation or Exposition?

Most college writing courses, and most of the standard rhetoric and composition textbooks, are organized around a central dichotomy: exposition, or expository writing, versus argumentative writing. Exposition is defined as writing that simply tells, informs, or explains, as opposed to writing that is trying to make a point or persuade someone. Technically speaking, most of the "rhetorical modes" that we learn in school, like narration, description, process, and comparison/contrast, fall under the heading of exposition: telling a story, explaining how things look or work or how they're alike or different.

There's just one problem with that model, and Aristotle himself nailed it over 2,500 years ago: in a practical sense, there's really no such thing as exposition. As Aristotle put it, "all public discourse is persuasive." By "discourse," I think we can understand him to mean "communication," so we're really talking about public communication. Of course, in Aristotle's day, the primary form of public communication was making speeches down at the Forum. To be sure, they did have the written word, but with no easy way to mass-publish documents—everything had to be copied over by hand—books were pretty rare and sources like newspapers and magazines basically unheard-of.

Obviously, today, we have many more forms of public communication, including the Internet, television, and radio, as well as magazines and newspapers—and even, occasionally, old-fashioned public speeches (especially in the political realm). But I'm pretty sure that Aristotle, if he could hop in the TARDIS with Dr. Who and visit our day (excuse my inner nerd), would still recognize all of these as forms of public discourse—and the same rule would apply. It's all, he would say, persuasive. Because his main point was that putting your ideas out there to the public is itself a form of persuasion.

Was he right? Well, let's test his theory by examining a type of public communication that, on the surface, might seem to be just giving information: the news. Yes, I know we're all very skeptical nowadays about political news being slanted, as well we should be. But what about plain old, old-fashioned news, like the car wreck that's causing the traffic jam you're sitting in or the robbery gone bad that left one dead and two wounded? Isn't that just information?

Before we go any further, let's take a moment and acknowledge that, if we allow for intent—that is, what the writer is trying to accomplish—then the exposition/argumentation distinction might have some validity. In that case, exposition would be defined as writing in which the author is just trying to convey information, whereas argumentation would be defined as writing by which the author hopes to persuade us of something. That makes sense, and it is probably the basis of the classic dichotomy.

There are just two problems with using intent as our litmus test. One is that, generally speaking, what actually happens is more important than what we intended. If you say something that hurts the feelings of someone close to you, it doesn't really matter that you didn't mean to. The fact is, you did. It happened. The other problem with using intent as our test is that we can never really be certain what someone intends. Heck, half the time, we're not even sure what we intend, much less what someone else intends. And trust me when I say that there are plenty of clever, competent, experienced arguers out there ready and willing to take advantage of that fact—people who understand very well that you're more likely to be persuaded if they present their ideas as just "the facts," rather than as the opinion it really is.

With that in mind, let's go back to the news. I'd like to tell you a true story that I believe illustrates my point (and Aristotle's).

Case Study: A Tragic Accident

Years ago, I lived in a very small town—so small that we didn't even have our own radio station or daily newspaper. Our local paper was published once in a week, on Thursday. Actually, I lived just south of town, and each morning on my way to work, I had to cross over the main east-west thoroughfare that passed through that part of the state, U.S. Highway 84. There was a stop sign there, but normally, crossing wasn't a problem because—well, it was a very small town. There was hardly any traffic. (Nowadays, living in the Atlanta suburbs, I sometimes long for those days. But I digress.)

The section of U.S. 84 just to the west of my little town was (and probably still is) notoriously dangerous—narrow and hilly and winding. It seemed like two or three times a year, there was a bad accident west of town, on that treacherous stretch of road.

One Tuesday morning, on my way to work, I pulled up to the stop sign at U.S. 84 and saw that the traffic going from east to west was backed up as far as I could see, while there was no one coming from the west. Naturally, I concluded that one of those bad accidents had occurred somewhere to the west. When I got to the college, I talked with others who had seen the bad traffic or been caught in it, and who were likewise speculating about what had happened. One guy had heard that several people had been killed. Another said she'd heard that one of our students was involved. But we didn't know. We had no radio station to issue traffic reports. We had to wait until the paper came out on Thursday.

Sure enough, on Thursday, there it was: a front page story about a horrific accident on U.S. 84, in which a nineteen-year-old kid (who was in fact one of our students) had collided head-on with another car driven by a young father with three small children. Tragically, the father and all three children had died at the scene, and the young man had been life-flighted to the nearest big-city hospital, where he remained in a coma and was not expected to live. The story didn't exactly come right out and say it, but it clearly implied that the college student was at fault.

Collectively, as a community, we all read that story and said to ourselves, "Oh. That's what happened. That is so sad." Many of us older adults might have even gone a step further and thought, "Those darned teenage drivers. They're a menace." But wait. How did we know that? Did we really know what happened? Or did we only know what we had been told? And if we read that story and concluded that we DID know what happened, were we not then persuaded—regardless of whether or not that's what the reporter intended?

In fairness, we must assume that reporter was doing her very best just to report on this terrible accident. She was probably young, in her first job out of college. She was probably lying there asleep that morning when her phone rang at 6:00 a.m. and her editor told her to get her rear end over to U.S. 84 west of town and cover the story. So she rolled out of bed, threw on a sweatshirt, and made her way over to the scene. She had to park half a mile away, because the traffic was so backed up, and when she finally got to the site of the accident, what did she see? Mangled cars. Dead bodies covered with sheets. People milling around—police, fire and rescue personnel, and bystanders. So she started doing her job: talking to all those people, or as many as she could corral, trying to find out what happened. And once she decided she had learned everything she could, she took her notes back to her desk and wrote the story we would eventually read, on Thursday.

But as she wrote, she realized she wasn't going to be able to put everything in the story; the paper wasn't going to give her that much space. So she made some decisions about what we, the reading public, really needed to know. Then her editor came along and made some more decisions, cut more out of the story. Note that we, the eventual readers, didn't get to decide what was important about the event—others made those decisions for us.

Let's go back for a moment to the reporter as she gathered information at the scene. Did she actually learn everything there was to learn? Is that even humanly possible? Probably not. So the information she had was, from the beginning, merely a subset of all the pertinent information. And then she whittled that down further, based on her assessment of we really needed to know and what we didn't. And yet, we read that story and concluded that we now knew what had happened.

In fact, we did not know what had happened; we only knew what we had been told.

What makes this story interesting, and the reason I tell it here at such length, is what came next. It seems the mother of the young man—who was still in a coma, clinging to life—became distraught, not only because her son was gravely injured but because everyone believed he was responsible for the deaths of four people, including three children! For her part, she was not convinced that her son was at fault, as the news story implied and as everyone now seemed to believe. So she launched an investigation of her own, talking to the highway patrol, reinterviewing the witnesses named in the news story, and finding two more people who claimed to be eye-witnesses and who told a very different story. The following week, the newspaper published a long letter to the editor from this woman, who made a very compelling case that her son was not to blame—that the accident had been the other driver's fault.

Week Three of the drama (if you've never lived in a small town, this is exactly what it's like): the newspaper published a follow-up in which they did not exactly retract the original story, but they did re-examined all the evidence—what their reporter had learned the day of the accident along with new evidence the mother had uncovered over the ensuing week—and concluded that . . . drum roll, please . . . no one really knew what had happened. It was impossible to determine who was to blame. And in fact, that young man, who eventually recovered, was never charged in the accident. There wasn't enough evidence to say it was his fault.

And yet, when we all read that initial story, we were completely convinced that it was. In taking that story at face value, we weren't merely informed, as we assumed; we were persuaded. That's what Aristotle meant when he said that all public discourse is persuasive.

But what about that reporter's intent? She wasn't really trying to persuade us of anything, was she? Wasn't she just trying, to the best of her ability, to tell us what happened?

Let's assume that's true—but remember what I said about intent. If the end result was that we came to believe something that, as it turns out, might not have been true, does it really matter if that was her intent or not? And how can we really know what she intended? What if we learned later that, five years earlier, her brother had been killed by a teenage drunk driver? Might that tragedy have influenced the way she perceived the events and reported the story? Would we as readers know that? Would she even necessarily be aware of her own bias in that instance?

The answer to those last two questions, obviously, is "no." And that is the essential problem with assuming that anyone is merely informing us. It's much safer, and usually more accurate, to assume that any messages aimed at us are intended to persuade—and that, when we share messages with others, we're doing the same thing.

What is Persuasion?

Perhaps, at this point, it would be useful to define the term "persuasion." So here's a handy-dandy pocket definition that applies in most situations:

Persuasion occurs when one person's perception influences another's.

My experience suggests that people (especially my students) generally find that definition unsatisfactory. They think it's a little weak—what they really want to hear is something like "changing people's opinions," not just influencing their perceptions. Because that's what we usually think of when we hear the word "persuasion": changing people's minds. You're going to the movies with your friends, and they all want to see one particular flick but you want to see a different one, so you talk them into coming with you. You changed their minds. That's persuasion—or so we think.

Honestly, though, how often do people change their minds—not about insignificant things, like which movie to see on Friday night, but about really important things, like religious beliefs, political opinions, or moral views? Yes, people do change their minds, even about things like that, but typically not very quickly, and not just because someone talked them into it. If that is the bar for persuasion—changing people's minds more or less instantaneously—then it rarely happens. Yet, as Aristotle observed, it's happening all the time. Therefore, the threshold must be quite a bit lower. Persuasion is usually more gradual and incremental. It's about influence over time.

Likewise, persuasion has more to do with perception than with opinion. What's the difference? That's kind of a trick question, because they're actually closely related. But let me take a stab at it: Everything—everything we think, everything we know, everything we think we know—is a perception. When we recognize it as such, as call it opinion. The rest of the time, we call it "fact." But obviously, there is a huge gray area. So much of what people regard as facts are actually just opinions or beliefs. When I was in school, there were nine planets in our solar system; that wasn't just a fact, it was the highest form of fact—a "scientific fact" (they all said reverently). Then, one day, it wasn't a fact anymore. Pluto was stripped of its planetary status. Now I hear that some scientists are calling it a planet (or a "dwarf planet") again, although others disagree. Either way, whether or not Pluto is a planet comes down to opinion—educated opinion based on facts, perhaps, but opinion nevertheless.

Ultimately, what we believe about Pluto depends on whose arguments we find most persuasive—and that has always been the case, even back when Pluto's planethood was simply an "accepted fact." Aristotle was right: it all comes down to persuasion, influencing people's perceptions over time. The good news is that we can do exactly that. We can influence people's perceptions and thus their opinions over time. That's how researchers have convinced millions of people to stop smoking or drive more fuel efficient vehicles.

I tell you all these things for two reasons. First, I want you to understand what the professional arguers, like politicians and advertisers and even scientists, are trying to do to you. They know they might not get you to change your mind overnight about which party you vote for, which brand of shampoo you use, or what kind of car you drive, but over time they believe they have a good chance of influencing your perceptions and therefore your behavior. So they keep at it, plugging away, like the steady drip of a faucet.

The other reason I'm telling you this is to help you understand, as an arguer yourself, both what you're up against and the power you have. You can indeed change people's minds, sometimes very quickly—especially if they're not already committed to a particular point of view—but more often slowly, incrementally, as you work to influence their perception and bring it more in line with your own. That is the essence of persuasion.

Aristotle's Means of Persuasion

So how do we do that—influence people's perceptions? Aristotle said there are three main ways, which he called Pathos, Ethos, and Logos. Logos, of course, has to do with logic, a chain of reasoning in which each point follows naturally from the one before and all of them together make perfect rational sense. Logic, in my view, is the most important of the three. Extended arguments aimed at sophisticated audiences should always be based primarily on logic. In fact, being able to persuade people using logical reasoning is so important that I'm going to devote the entire next chapter to that topic. For now, though, I'll set that aside and talk about the other two.

Note that I said logic is the most important of the three means of persuasion—not the only one. Too many logic teachers seem to believe that any reasoning that is not strictly logical is therefore bad or unethical or immoral. I don't agree with that point of view, and I don't think Aristotle did, either. Why else would he bother identifying and explaining the other two?

Note, too, my statement that "extended arguments for sophisticated audiences should be based primarily on logic." "Primarily" is not the same as "solely." Furthermore, not all arguments are extended—long speeches or pieces of writing. Sometimes, as in television commercials, arguers have only seconds to persuade their audience. For that matter, to be blunt, not all audiences are "sophisticated." Clearly, the politicians and advertisers seem to be convinced that most of us aren't very sophisticated, because they rarely base their arguments primarily on logic.

What I'm saying is that it's not wrong for them to do so. As arguers, they have at their disposal every tool—except for outright deception, which of course IS immoral. But beyond that, if they can persuade you by manipulating your emotions in a way that's not strictly logical, I would say that's your problem, not theirs. That's why I spent the first four chapters of this book talking about how to use your brain, evaluate information, and think things through—precisely so you won't be led around by the nose, a slave to your emotions.

More to the point, as an arguer, you have these same tools at your disposal. Let's look at them more closely, and remember—we'll spend a lot more time talking about logic in the next chapter.

Pathos: Emotional Appeal

The Greek root "path"—not to be confused with the Anglo-Saxon word referring to a trail or walkway—has to do with the emotions. To be a "pathological" liar means to tell lies without any emotional consequences (namely, guilt). To have "sympathy" for someone means to feel the same emotions as that person. And so on.

What Aristotle called "pathos," then, can be translated for our day as "emotional appeal" or, perhaps more accurately, "appeal to emotion." Aristotle understood very well that, as we discussed in earlier chapters, humans are emotional beings, often motivated more by their feelings than by logic or reason. If we want to persuade people to do things, then, it just makes sense that one very effective means of accomplishing that is by appealing to their emotions.

It should go without saying that emotional appeal is not logical; it's practically the exact opposite. However, as I noted above, that doesn't mean there's anything morally wrong with it. As I said, emotional appeal is a weapon that all arguers have, or ought to have, in their arsenal. If the targets of those appeals, the members of the audience, are motivated to act strictly based on emotions—if they fail to think things through and apply at least a little bit of logic to the situation—then I would say that's their failure. Once again, one of the reasons I'm telling you these things is so you'll understand what the professional arguers are constantly doing to you and thus be better equipped to resist and counter those arguments when they are not, in fact, logical. As they say, forewarned is forearmed. But the other reason I'm telling you about emotional appeal, in particular, is so that you can use it, selectively, in your own arguments.

After all, some of the most effective arguments we encounter are based primarily if not solely on emotional appeal. Politicians, for example, use it all the time. Have you ever noticed how little time politicians spend, these days, arguing why people should vote for them, as opposed to the time they spend arguing why people should NOT vote for their opponent? The message is, "You might not like me much, but you simply cannot vote for him/her, because—Oh my gosh!—he/she will do all these terrible things," like take away your social security benefits, starve the children, put an end to employee-provided insurance, set us on the road to socialism—you fill in the blank. Most of the time, those arguments are not really logical; it's unlikely any one politician could do any of those things if he or she tried. But they are emotionally powerful. They make people afraid, and fear is probably the strongest emotion when it comes to motivating people to act.

And then there are the advertisers, who rely heavily on emotional appeal for two reasons: they are not making extended arguments, and they don't consider us a very sophisticated audience. (Politicians rely on pathos mostly for the latter reason.) Unfortunately, for us, they're probably right—we aren't very sophisticated, if that means applying our brains rather than simply being led by our feelings. All their market research suggests that's true. And so they offer absurd reasons why we should want to use their products—like the men's deodorant spray commercial from a few years ago in which scantily clad models literally fell out of the sky and landed at the feet of the guy who used the product.

We might think a commercial like that is using sex—more specifically, the emotion of lust—to sell its products, and that is true to a degree. But once again, the emotion they're really appealing to is fear. Because the message is actually a negative one. The point is not so much that if you use their product, you'll be attractive to potential mates; it's that, if you don't buy their product—if you don't use their brand of deodorant, or drink their brand of beer, or drive their brand of car—no one will find you attractive. You will probably die old and alone. As silly as that may sound, it speaks to a primal fear, and advertisers know it.

When I was a young father, there was a popular brand of tires whose commercials featured a smiling, happy baby gliding along inside one of their products. The message was not so much, "If you drive on our brand of tires, your family will be safe"; rather, it was, "If you DON'T drive on our brand of tires, you're putting your entire family at risk." Millions of us looked at those commercials, thought to ourselves, "Gee, I've got a smiling, happy little baby of my own. I better buy some new tires if I want to keep her safe!" Believe me, they sold a lot of tires that way.

Again, that's not logical. A logical approach would be to ask yourself, first, "Do I need new tires?" If the answer is "no," then your next thought might be, "When I do need new tires, I'll be sure to check out that brand." If the answer is "yes, I need new tires," then the rational approach would be to research tire brands—cost and stopping distances and wear factors—and decide if that one is right for you. Perhaps you find it's more expensive than some of its competitors but decide, based on your research, that it's worth it. That's a logical conclusion, consistent with the evidence. Or perhaps you decide that, even though that brand is a little better, another brand is almost as good and fits your budget. That, too, is a logical conclusion. The point is that you did your homework and thought it through. But just buying a set of expensive tires because you're afraid of what might happen to your baby if you don't? That's not logical.

Yet it's undeniably powerful. And my message, in addition to warning you about these emotional attacks being launched against you on a daily basis, is that you can also harness the same power in your own arguments. Understanding that extended arguments for sophisticated audiences should be based primarily on logic, you must be careful how you use emotional appeal—and how much of it you use. Too much pathos will likely make sophisticated readers (or listeners) feel like they're being emotionally manipulated, mostly because they're being emotionally manipulated. But a little bit of emotional appeal, especially right up front, can have the effect of softening up your readers—moving them slightly in your direction emotionally before you start to appeal to their reason.

Let's say you're writing an impassioned plea to strengthen gun control laws, but your argument consists entirely of anecdotes about heart-wrenching incidents of gun violence—the honor student killed in a drive-by on her way home from the library, the grandmother hit by a stray bullet while watching television in her living room, the little boy who found his father's loaded pistol and accidentally shot his brother to death. At some point, after several of those stories, an intelligent, perceptive reader will likely stop and say, "Wait a second. You're just yanking my chain. Where's the meat of your argument? Where are the statistics and other pieces of factual evidence?" They'll feel like you're just manipulating their emotions, not making a cohesive logical argument.

But what if you start off your argument with, say, just one of those stories—maybe the most heart-wrenching one—and then you segue from that right into your factual evidence? That could actually be a pretty effective means of making an argument. A little bit of pathos, used selectively and in small doses, can sway your audience emotionally so they're more inclined to listen to what you have to say. But too much can have the opposite effect.

Ethos: Image Appeal

Another effective (if not exactly logical) means of making an argument is what Aristotle called "ethos." That sounds like it might have something to do with ethics (and in fact, it does), but it can best be translated as "appeal to image," or maybe "appeal from image." Simply put, ethos as to do with credibility. The basic premise is that people are more likely to believe the argument if they believe the *arguer*—if they find him or her to be credible.

As a child of the 1960s and 1970s, I've occasionally been amused to see guys elected to Congress who, back when I was kid, were well-known campus radicals, running around in sandals and love beads with hair down to the middle of their back. In many cases, their politics haven't changed that much, if at all. They just figured out, at some point, that they weren't going to get elected to Congress with long hair, wearing sandals and love beads. They had to get a conservative haircut, put on a dark suit and tie, and look just like every other politician—because that's what voters expect. It has to do with the image they project.

There's a great scene in the movie *Adjustment Bureau* in which a guy running for Senate, played by Matt Damon, stops in the middle of stump speech, takes off one of his black dress shoes, and holds it up for the crowd. "Do you realize," he tells them (and I'm paraphrasing somewhat here), "that I have people who tell me exactly how scuffed my shoes should be? If they're too scuffed, I look like I'm down and out, and nobody wants to vote for somebody like that. But if they're too shiny, then I look like some sort of rich, out-of-touch elitist, and nobody wants to vote for somebody like that, either. For me to be elected, my shoes have to have just the right amount of scuffing."

What the Matt Damon character is talking about is what Aristotle called ethos—attempting to project exactly the right image so that, when we make arguments, our audience is more likely to believe us. Politicians do this constantly, out of necessity.

They're not the only ones. Advertisers do it, too, often using famous spokespeople that we already like and admire. Honestly, what does Michael Jordan know about men's underwear that the rest of us don't? Probably nothing. But when he shoots a Hanes commercial, it makes us (us guys, at least) want to buy Hanes underwear, because we like Michael Jordan and on some level want to be like him.

And that's really what ethos is all about: drawing the audience to the person making the argument, essentially presenting them with a reflection of themselves as they would like to be. As they see themselves, deep down. Guys look at Michael Jordan and think, "I may not be as tall as Michael Jordan, or as handsome as Michael Jordan, or as good at basketball as Michael Jordan—but I'm kinda tall, kinda handsome, kinda good at sports. And hey, there's at least one thing I can do just like Michael Jordan—wear Hanes underwear!" There's some powerful psychology involved in that mental process, even though it's not exactly rational.

The "image" doesn't even have to be anyone famous. Back in the 1960s, there was a brand of cigarette that was near the bottom of the sales charts. So the manufacturer hired a new advertising firm, and they came up with a brilliant campaign: the Marlboro Man—a ruggedly handsome cowboy, perched on horseback, with the snow-capped Rocky Mountains in the background. Within a couple of years, Marlboro cigarettes had vaulted to near the top of the sales charts, all because that advertising agency managed to capture an image that resonated with people (especially men) across the country.

Indeed, the Marlboro Man quickly became iconic. Through him, the advertisers reached out to millions of grown men who were still, at heart, little boys—who still wanted to grow up to be a cowboy. As adults, with jobs and families and mortgages, what were they going to do to finally realize that dream—sell everything, move to Montana, and buy a ranch? Of course not. But there was one thing they could do: They could smoke Marlboro cigarettes. And they did, by the millions. That's the power of image appeal.

For us, as writers—as arguers—image appeal is equally vital. Whereas emotional appeal, or pathos, is a tool to be used carefully and selectively, ethos is something we should always be attempting to harness to our advantage. We should always be trying, when we make arguments, to present ourselves in the best possible light. Remember: People are much more likely to believe the argument if they trust the arguer. One of our main jobs, as arguers, is to get people to trust us so they're more likely to believe us.

How do we do that? Well, in person we dress nicely (like for a job interview or a presentation) and behave courteously. But what about in writing, especially when our audience consists of people we've never met? How do we establish credibility with those readers?

Let me suggest a couple of things. First, going back to our discussion about "good writing" in Chapters 5–8, we should do our best to use good grammar, write clear sentences, and organize our ideas so people can follow us. We should also go out of our way to be engaging and accessible. Remember, readers are going to make judgments about us based on the way we write; ethos is about making sure those judgments are positive ones.

Beyond that, we can take time to do our homework so that we come across as knowledgeable and well-informed. We can be measured in our tone, not ranting and raving or making statements that are obviously exaggerated or simply not true. Perhaps you've had the experience of reading something you essentially agreed with—but the way the writer presented it repelled you, to the point where you almost wanted to disagree. It just seemed completely over the top. Conversely, you may have read something with which you fundamentally disagreed—but which was so well written, and sounded so reasonable, that you found yourself wanting to agree. That, too, demonstrates the power of ethos.

Overt versus Covert Arguments

Up to this point, I've been using the words "argument" and "persuasion" more or less interchangeably. But they're not exactly the same thing. If Aristotle was correct (and I believe he was), then all public communication is persuasive, whether we intend it to be or not. Argumentation is when you do it on purpose—when you actively set out to persuade an audience. Hence, harking back to our earlier discussion about exposition and argumentation, we could say that there are two types of persuasion, unintentional and intentional. The latter is what we call argumentation.

But there are also two types of arguments, which we'll call overt and covert. Overt, of course, means "open" or "obvious." Thus, overt argumentation occurs when the arguer essentially says, in very straightforward terms, "Here's what I'm trying to persuade you of, and here's my evidence." This is the most common type of argument professionals make, and it is practically the only type of argument academics make, so clearly it's important for educated people to know how do it effectively. Fortunately, you've almost certainly had some experience in making overt arguments already, since nearly all of our academic training focuses on that type. Plus, I'm going to devote the entire next section to talking about it.

But there is another type of argument that we don't talk about as much, and that is covert arguments. "Covert" means "hidden" or "secret," like a "covert agent" in a spy novel. Covert arguments, then, are arguments that people make without disclosing to their audience that they're actually making an argument. Often, the argument is disguised as something else, like straight news or a fictional narrative or even an argument for something else entirely. Even if you've never thought of it in quite that way, you no doubt understand intuitively that such arguments exist; that's why we've become so distrustful of news sources, for instance—because we suspect that, in many cases, they're not just giving us information. They're actually making a covert argument.

In the news business, that approach is considered suspect at best and downright unethical at worst, even though it happens all the time. We could make a good case that arguments disguised as news—"just the facts, ma'am," in the words of the immortal Elwood Blues (Google him)—have become more common today than actual news. That's because professional arguers, whether in the media or in politics or in advertising, know very well that we're more likely to believe what they say if they frame it as information rather than acknowledging, up front, that it's just their perspective.

But that doesn't mean covert argumentation is inherently unethical, or that we can't put it to good use as arguers. It's another tool in our toolbox, to be used carefully and selectively, in a considered, thoughtful manner—but used, nonetheless. There's obviously a time and a place to take the direct, overt approach, to say to your audience, in essence, "Okay, folks, here's what I think and here's why." But just as obviously, there are times when that might NOT be the best approach—when it could actually hurt your cause rather than help it. There are times when it's to your advantage, as an arguer, to hold back your thesis, or even the fact that you're making an argument at all, as long as possible.

Imagine walking into a conference room, faced with the daunting task of presenting an unpopular decision to the people who work for you. Should you simply bite the bullet and come right out with it? Maybe. There are certainly times that might be the best approach. It depends, to some extent, on the people in the room and on the decision itself. Some things simply can't be sugar-coated. But what if, by coming at your argument from a different angle, you could actually achieve some buy-in, early on, from the folks in the room? Not by lying to them or tricking them, but simply by presenting the information in way that's more palatable, or at least that won't provoke immediate anger and resistance. If your objective is to persuade, that could definitely make your argument more effective.

One good way to disguise an argument is to weave it into a narrative—essentially, to tell a story. That actually takes us back to the concept of pathos, because it's not strictly logical and the story will almost certainly have an emotional component. That's kind of the point. But the story will also be designed to help readers (or, in our hypothetical situation, the people in that conference room) see for themselves the truth of the matter, as opposed to your having to state it baldly up front and risk riling people up or having them tune you out.

At times, you might just use a story to lead into your argument and then make the case more straightforwardly from there. At other times, you might want to let the story become your argument, approaching the issue more subtly as readers become immersed in the narrative. I read an opinion piece in the *New York Times* several years by a novelist named Marc Fitten. Writing not long after the Great Recession began in 2008, Marc told a story about visiting a local high-end home decor retailer and finding the items there still priced beyond reach—even though no one could now afford them. Not long after, that store went out of business. He concluded that the economy had collapsed because it was always doomed to collapse. It was a house of cards. For years, people had been buying things they couldn't really afford, paying for them with credit. Now, in the throes of recession, credit was hard to come by, people were no longer buying those items, and the retailers were feeling the pain. It was a very thought-provoking piece about the human behavioral causes of the recession.

But imagine, for a moment, if Marc had simply said, up front, "Here's why I think the economy collapsed." Can you imagine the push-back he might have gotten? "That's not why." "You don't know what you're talking about." "You're not even an economist." (He's not.) Many of those readers wouldn't have gotten past the first sentence or two, much less made it to the meat of his argument. So instead of taking that approach, which would have been extremely ineffective, he went at it from a different angle. He told a story about a personal experience, but one that most readers could relate to. Before they even understood what he was arguing, readers got caught up in the narrative. By the time they realized what he was really saying—well, they could still disagree, but they had already read it! And I imagine many of them found it compelling and were at least somewhat persuaded to modify their own perception.

That's an effective argument.

Another way to argue covertly is to say the exact opposite of what you intend to argue—initially, at least. In its simplest form, we call this sarcasm; when it's more sophisticated, we call it satire. But both of those have essentially the same effect: You're saying one thing while actually meaning another. At some point, whether early on or much later, that fact becomes apparent to the reader or listener, and the stark contrast between what you claim to be arguing and what you're actually arguing helps drive home your point.

There's a very famous feminist essay from the early 1970s called "I Want a Wife," by Judy Syfers Brady. In that piece, Brady talks about her life as a wife and mother who also, apparently, works outside the home. She details all the things she does in that capacity—taking care of the children, cooking the meals, doing the laundry, attending to her husband's personal needs, and so forth (there's quite a list). Meanwhile, her husband, who appears to be in graduate or professional school, basically does nothing except go to school. According to Brady, she takes care of pretty much everything in the home. She concludes that she wishes SHE had a wife to do all those things for her, so she wouldn't have to do them.

Of course, we don't for a moment assume that Brady is saying she'd actually like to marry a woman and have a literal wife. That's not the point. The point she's making is that women in our society were (and perhaps still are, to some extent) treated very differently from men. They're expected to set aside their own wants and needs in order to take care of their husbands, children, and homes. It's a powerful argument for gender equality, even though that's not the way it's framed, initially.

Another example is Jonathan Swift's classic satirical essay, "A Modest Proposal," in which he suggests that wealthy, eighteenth-century English landlords should actually eat—yes, eat—the children of their poor Irish tenants: "A young, healthy child well-nursed is at a year old a most delicious, nourishing, and wholesome food." Of course he doesn't mean that literally (even though it sounds, for several paragraphs, like he does). His point is that, the way those rich, out-of-touch folks were mistreating their tenants, they might as well eat the babies; it wouldn't be much worse than what they'd already done, which was to consign them to a life of poverty. That becomes obvious later in the essay, when Swift says, "I grant this food will be somewhat dear [or expensive] and therefore very proper for landlords, who, as they have already devoured most of the parents, seem to have the best title to the children."

Essentially, Swift was "calling out" those wealthy landlords, chastising them for their horrible treatment of their tenants and ultimately trying to persuade them to be more just and compassionate. What made his argument effective—to the extent it was effective; history suggests the behavior of the English toward the

Irish didn't improve much—or at least what made it memorable, was the scandalous sensationalism of his ostensible thesis: Let's eat babies. That both repulsed readers and, in an odd way, drew them in, making them want to see exactly where this dude was coming from. In the process, they discovered his real thesis—we need to treat these people better—and could not help but be moved by it, even if only a little bit.

Thesis, Support, and Refutation

All of that said, there aren't many opportunities to use satire or even story-telling in academic or professional arguments. (I wish there were, because it can be fun.) Even so, it's still valuable to know how to utilize those strategies. Acknowledging that we might not pull them out and dust them off very often is not the same as saying we'll never use them. Plus, other people, like comics, essayists, and script writers, do in fact use those very strategies to influence us, so it's worthwhile to understand how they work.

Still, most of the arguments we make, in both academic and professional life, will take a much more straightforward, thesis-and-support approach, in which we state right up front what we're arguing and then offer evidence to back it up. Another strategy that sometimes comes into play, and which I also want to talk about in this section, is called refutation, making a case for your point of view by arguing against the other side. That is often (although not always) an important part of a thesis-and-support argument. Let's discuss each of these elements in a little more detail.

Thesis. Simply put, your thesis is what you're arguing. It's the main point of your essay—or report or proposal or narrative or whatever vehicle you're using to make your argument.

We should distinguish, however, between "thesis" and another term that's often used in high school and college "language arts" classes (but hardly anywhere else): "thesis *statement*." A thesis statement is, as the term suggests, a statement of your thesis—a sentence or two that sums up your main point. It usually (but not always) appears near the beginning of the argument, in the first or second paragraph. Its primary purpose is to let readers know, right up front, what you're arguing, what you intend to show them based on the evidence that follows. As we've seen, that is often an effective strategy: "Here's what I think, and here's why."

We've also seen, though, that it's not always an effective strategy. Sometimes, the best approach is to disguise your thesis, or not reveal it right away, or allow your readers to infer it on their own. That's why, although every argument has a thesis, pretty much by definition, not every argument has a clear, easily identifiable thesis statement—a single passage that sums up the thesis. Sometimes it's better to do it that way, and sometimes it's better to take a more round-about approach.

For your sake as writer, though, whether you state your thesis outright or not, you should always know what it is—what you are basically trying to argue. Most of the bad arguments I've read or heard, from students as well as people who ought to know better, suffer from the absence of a clear thesis. The writers simply don't know what they're trying to say, and as a result, they have a great deal of trouble saying it—and as readers, we have just as much trouble following it. Or maybe they started out knowing what they wanted to say but found themselves drifting, getting sidetracked, or following rabbit trails. I'm often guilty of that myself, especially when I'm writing something that's on the long side, like a journal article or book chapter. I've found that it helps to jot my thesis down somewhere, in very simple terms, even if that exact phrase ultimately doesn't appear anywhere in what I'm writing. Then, when I find myself getting off-track, I can go back and remind myself what I originally set out to say.

In fact, that's a secondary reason for having a thesis to begin with. Ultimately, it serves the readers by helping them understand where you're coming from. But initially it serves you, as a steady reminder of where you're headed.

Support. I'm not going to say a lot about support at this point, because I plan to spend the entire last section of this chapter talking about it. Suffice it to say, for now, that what I mean by "support" is the evidence you're citing to back up your thesis. It's the "why" part of the sentence above: "Here's what I think, and here's *why.*"

As we learned back in Chapter 4, an argument without any evidence is not an argument at all; it's merely an assertion. That's essentially what a thesis is: an assertion. Only evidence—aka, support—can turn it into an actual argument. In the next section, we'll see what kinds of supporting evidence you can offer to convince your readers that your thesis is true—and thereby stand a better chance of actually persuading them.

Refutation. The last thing I want to talk about in this section is a rhetorical strategy known as "refutation" or sometimes "rebuttal." This strategy begins with an understanding that arguments do not exist in a vacuum; they are always dialog, not monolog. An argument never involves just one person, flapping their gums to an empty room. There's always at least one other side to the argument, perhaps many other sides. Otherwise, it wouldn't be an argument. We would all just agree, hold hands, sing "Kumbyah," and go home. Ignoring the other side or pretending that it doesn't exist is rarely a winning strategy. Much better to acknowledge it and deal with it. That's what we call "refutation."

Imagine you're walking into a conference room to give the biggest presentation of your life, arguing in front of your boss and coworkers that the company needs to invest in some expensive new piece of software. You've run all the numbers and can show how much money it will save the company over the next five years. The problem is, the program really is pretty expensive. So, should you acknowledge that fact in your presentation, or try to gloss over it? Our tendency as human beings is often to do the latter—to attempt to ignore or downplay those factors that might not seem to support our point of view. Unfortunately, we often do so at our own peril.

Let's say there are ten people in that conference room. A couple of them are your buddies. Maybe they even helped you put the presentation together. But there are bound to be one or two people in the room who are your enemies, or at least work rivals. They want to see you fail, either because they support (or put forward) an alternative proposal or just because they have it in for you. What if you try to gloss over the fact that this new software is going to cost over a million dollars? Don't you think one of those "enemies" is going to bring up that point, probably at the most inopportune moment? And you'll be left standing up at the front of the room, stammering, "Well, um, I, uh . . . ." Not good.

But what if you brought up that piece of information yourself? What if you pointed out the cost in one of your early slides? "As you can see, our initial outlay will be substantial. About a million dollars. However, my projections show—next slide, please—that we'll save more than six million dollars over the next five years." Now what does that person, your enemy, have left to say? Nothing. You've essentially disarmed them, simply by bringing up that point yourself and then refuting it—showing why it's not a good reason to reject your argument.

What this strategy requires, obviously, is that you know what the other side is likely to say. In some cases, that's pretty obvious or at least easily predictable—just ask yourself what you would say if you were on their side—but at other times, you may really have to do your homework. It's worth it, though, if you can essentially disarm your opponents (and remember, there are always opponents) by bringing up their points before they do and dismissing them before they can hurt you. Great arguers throughout the ages have used this strategy to great effect, from Thomas Paine in *Common Sense* to Dr. King in his "Letter from a Birmingham Jail." (If you're serious about learning to make effective arguments, I highly recommend that you read both of those.)

There are several ways to refute the other side. The best way is to show that they are simply wrong—that their assumptions are not supported by evidence, that their supposed facts are not facts at all. Failing that, perhaps you can show that, even if technically correct, their arguments are irrelevant to the issue at hand: "That may be true, but so what? What does that have to do with this discussion?" Perhaps you can show that the other side's arguments may be true up to a point, but they don't extend to the situation you're addressing. Or maybe you can demonstrate that their evidence is incomplete. It may be true, as presented, but they've left out important information that would completely change the conclusion. Any of those will cast doubt on their arguments and thereby strengthen your own.

Supporting Your Thesis

As I said, there are lots of ways to support your thesis. In fact, before I go on, this might be a good time to point out that, in this chapter, I have barely scratched the surface when it comes to making good arguments. Entire books, much longer than this one, have been written on that topic alone. There are many other rhetorical strategies out there, and more to be said about the ones I did touch on. However, I do believe that, by following the advice in this book, you will become a more effective arguer or at least begin your journey down that road. I've tried to frame these topics in a way that is concise, easily grasped, and immediately useful.

I recommend, however, that you continue your education by reading other books about making arguments, along with examples of great arguments put forward by skilled arguers. Those can often be found in the pages (actual or virtual) of our nation's newspapers, in the form of op-eds ranging from politics to sports to entertainment. Not all of those arguments are good ones—perhaps you can use your budding analytical skills to evaluate their validity and effectiveness—but many of them are. You can also learn a lot about writing style from people like Leonard Pitts, Kathleen Parker, George Will, and Jason Whitlock, whether or not you agree with whatever they happen to be saying.

But I digress. I was saying that there are many ways to support a thesis, but in this final section of Chapter 9, I want to focus on four that I believe are fairly comprehensive and universal—meaning they apply to all types and styles of arguments.

Definition of terms. One of the first things you should do, in any argument, is define terms as necessary, for two reasons. First, as a practical matter, you want to make sure your readers understand what you're talking about. But also, it's a long-standing and well-known truism that the one who defines the terms usually wins the argument. If you can get readers to accept your definitions of key words and phrases, you've already taken a huge step toward persuading them. An obvious example of this can be found in the same-sex marriage debate from a few years ago. If supporters could convince the public that the word "marriage"—which for centuries referred exclusively to the union of a man and women—could also be applied to same-sex relationships, then it was only a matter of time before that new definition became codified into law.

When I talk about defining terms, I don't just mean words or phrases that most people might not know, although of course that's important. Examples of such language would include professional jargon and technical terms. "Jargon" refers to the kind of verbal shorthand that people in a given field, like medicine or education, often use among themselves. Usually, there are other, more common words that people not in those fields would use to describe the same things. "Technical terms" are just that—terms that describe technical phenomena and for which there are no other words. That's just what it's called.

When it comes to clear writing—not to mention making good arguments—a good rule is to avoid jargon as much as possible while defining technical terms as needed. For example, if I use a word like "assessment" in a newspaper column, for a general audience, I have to acknowledge that people who aren't professional educators—even smart, well-educated people in other fields—might not know exactly what it means. I need to define it for them. Or perhaps I could just say "testing" to begin with, since that's a term most readers would understand.

Just as important, however, is explaining to people what YOU mean by a particular word or phrase. They might know the dictionary definition but not understand how you're using it in context. For example, if I'm writing about my nosy neighbors, trying to convince readers that my neighbors really are the nosiest people ever (they're not—this is just a hypothetical), then I need to explain what I mean by "nosy." My readers obviously know what the word means, but they might not know what I mean when I use it. In what way are my neighbors nosy? What do they do that's so annoying? I probably need to explain, too, exactly what I mean by "neighbors." Everyone in my subdivision? The people in my cul-de-sac? Just my next-door neighbors? That kind of specific information is key to helping readers grasp—and be swayed by—my overall argument. For that reason, as arguers, we should always take great care to define terms as necessary—and as we want them to be understood.

Factual evidence. Another way to support a thesis—and perhaps the most important way—is by introducing factual evidence that indicates the thesis is true. That evidence can take various forms, including statements of fact by reliable, knowledgeable sources. If someone who knows a great deal about a topic makes a categorical statement in regard to that topic, we can generally accept it as fact. For example, when legendary college basketball coach Dean Smith says that missed shots taken from one side of the court usually come off on the other side, we can safely assume that's true and formulate our defensive strategy accordingly.

Factual evidence also includes (but is not limited to) statistics. Some caution is called for here, for reasons we will explore in the next chapter. Suffice it to say, for now, that not all statistics are created equal—and some are just that, created. Nevertheless, many are perfectly valid and can therefore go a long way toward demonstrating the accuracy of a given thesis. Also, as an arguer and connoisseur of arguments, I can't help but notice that people are suckers for statistics; if you want to persuade people, throw some numbers at them. Just make sure first that your numbers are accurate, relevant, and complete—that is, that they reflect the whole picture. Otherwise, you open yourself up to potential attacks. Remember, this is an argument, and there are people on the other side, just waiting for you to trip up so they can win the argument. But those caveats aside, you should by all means be looking for statistics that support your side of the argument. As I said, they can be extremely persuasive.

Expert testimony. We talked above about citing knowledgeable people, or experts, who may have a great deal of factual evidence to offer. But they also have opinions—opinions that may be based on facts, on years of study and experience, but which are nevertheless opinions, not statements of fact. That doesn't mean what those experts think—as opposed to what they know—can't also be persuasive. Whenever anyone who knows a lot about a topic makes some pronouncement regarding that topic, people have a tendency to listen, even if it's just their opinion.

For example, if Coach Smith says that he's studied the matter, and most rebounds come off on the opposite side of the basket, that's a fact. You can take it to the bank. But if he then says that, in response to this fact, defenders on the opposite side of the court should be closer to the basket than to the person they're guarding—well, that's his opinion. It's certainly an informed opinion, and one that any intelligent basketball coach interested in improving their team's performance would do well to consider. But it's still just an opinion. Other knowledgeable, successful coaches might take a different approach altogether.

When it comes to citing expert opinion, what you're essentially doing is allowing those highly credible sources to speak for you. The opinion they're expressing is really YOUR opinion; that's why you're including it in your argument, as a means of supporting your thesis. You're just allowing them to say it instead of saying it yourself, because—no offense—they know more about it than you do. They're more credible. Essentially, like an advertiser paying Michael Jordan to hawk their product, you're "borrowing" someone else's ethos. That in no way reflects badly on you. It doesn't mean you're stupid or ignorant. In fact, the opposite is true. Bolstering your own opinion with concurring opinions held by known experts positively enhances your argument. It's something that, as an arguer, you should always be trying to do.

Examples and case studies. The last strategy for supporting your thesis that I want to talk about in this chapter is using examples. Those can come from your own experience, from the experiences of others, of from your research. In all three cases, however, what examples accomplish—or at least, what they're intended to accomplish—is to illustrate your point for readers, to show them how it applies in real life.

There are actually three different types of examples: lists, anecdotes, and case studies. List are just that. If I say, "Now that we're empty-nesters, my wife and I are thinking about trading in the minivan for a sports car," you might respond, "Really? That's cool. What kind of sports car are you interested in?" And then I might reply, "Well, so far we've looked at the Mazda Miata and the little Pontiac two-seater. The Nissan 300z is really nice but a little expensive. And of course, who wouldn't like to have a Porsche if they could afford one?" Do you see what I did there? I listed several different vehicles as examples of what I meant when I used the term "sports car."

Another type of example is the anecdote, which is essentially a short narrative—a little story that, again, illustrates your point. For example, going back to my hypothetical discussion about my nosey neighbors, perhaps the best way for me to get readers to understand what I mean by "nosey" is to talk about something one my neighbors actually did—like the time the woman next door saw that we had company and so came over supposedly to borrow a cup of sugar but actually to see who was there. (Again—I'm making that up, but you get the point.) That's an anecdote. I could even use more than one anecdote if I really want to make my point, or if I'm concerned that one isn't enough.

The third type of example is actually an extended anecdote, a much longer narrative known as a case study. Case studies are sometimes hypothetical but are often based on actual events, although in many cases, the names and other details have been changed to protect people's privacy (and/or avoid lawsuits). Such extended anecdotes may, as I noted above, come from your own experience, but they are more likely to come up in your research. One of the things that makes case studies so powerful, as evidence, is that they tend to be rather clinical—that is, thoroughly analyzed by objective professionals—or at least give that appearance. You're not just saying, "Hey, I've noticed such-and-such happening." You're saying, "A bunch of professional researchers have observed such-and-such happening, and here's a clinical account of their observations."

The up-side of using examples, especially anecdotes and case studies, is that they really do have a powerful effect on readers. They truly illustrate your point, making it real in the minds of your readers, allowing them to experience it vicariously, to "see" it in their mind's eye (hence the word "illustrate"). For that reason, when making arguments, you should always be alert for opportunities to illustrate your points using examples. The truth is, some points don't really need examples; they have plenty of factual evidence to back them up. Other points, like the one about my nosey neighbors, are almost impossible to make without using examples. How else can I explain how annoying my neighbors are other than by showing you how they act? And then there are points you might be able to make without using examples, but which an example or two could definitely enhance. Those are the ones to keep an eye out for.

The downside of using examples is that, if you're not careful, you can be accused of relying too heavily on "anecdotal evidence." It is a truism of argumentation that anecdotal evidence, by itself, does not really mean much. It's like the guy who calls into the radio talk show to say that he's certain Candidate X is going to win the upcoming election because everyone in his neighborhood has a yard sign for Candidate X. As I'm sure you can see, that's basically meaningless. It's not even a real poll, much less a scientific one that takes multiple factors into account.

That's why it's important to always use examples in conjunction with other evidence—as a way of enhancing your point, not as your sole means of making it. If an example is your only evidence, readers can always say to themselves, "Well, that's all well and good, but that doesn't mean it applies to me." But when you make a strong case—defining terms, using factual evidence and expert testimony—then add an example to make the point come alive for your readers, to show them how it applies to real life, that can have a remarkable effect.

Details, details, details. What all these methods of supporting a thesis have in common is that they rely heavily on *details*. That's really the crux of the matter, when it comes to persuading people. How detailed are your definitions (as opposed to being vague)? How about the statistics you cite, or the expert testimony? And your examples—how detailed are they? Certainly, there is such a thing as too much detail ("TMI"); you have to balance the need for conciseness against a desire to recite every last, unimportant detail. In my experience, though, that's rarely a problem. Usually, arguers don't give enough detail, which can leave readers unconvinced. The key is to provide enough concrete details so that readers can understand both the point itself and how it relates to and ultimately supports your main point, your thesis. That's how you make an effective argument.

REFERENCES

Brady, Judy Syfers. "I Want a Wife." *New York Magazine*, December 1971.

Fitten, Marc. "Cushioning the Blow." *nytimes.com*. The New York Times. 7 March 2009.

Swift, Jonathan. "A Modest Proposal." *Gutenberg.org*. Project Gutenberg. 6 February 2013.

USING LOGIC AND REASON

This chapter is in many ways a continuation of Chapter 9. We could just as easily call it "Using Logic and Reason—to Make (and Win) Arguments." I decided to create a separate chapter for two reasons: so that no single chapter would become too long (Chapter 9 is plenty long already) and because I think logic is important enough to deserve its own chapter. In the interests of full disclosure, this chapter does re-examine some of the same concepts we talked about in Chapter 9 but from a different perspective, looking at how they relate to logic and reason.

Although logic and reason are closely related, they're not exactly the same thing. Logic is basically the application of the critical thinking skills we talked about extensively in the first several chapters. It is objective, analytical, fact-based, and dispassionate. Reason, on the other hand, goes a step further, incorporating factors that might not be logical but are, nevertheless, relevant. Back in Chapter 2, we learned that being "dispassionate" doesn't necessarily mean rejecting or ignoring our emotions altogether; rather, it means recognizing those emotions for what they are and giving them the weight they deserve. Depending on the situation, that might be a lot or it might be none at all. Likewise, we saw in the last chapter that there are emotion-based tools for persuasion—namely, pathos and ethos—that, although not strictly logical, are nonetheless quite effective. Reason is a thinking process that uses both logic and nonlogic to reach conclusions and, ultimately, make arguments.

The adjectival form of "reason," in this context, is "rational." We are rational beings, meaning we have the ability to use our brains in order to solve complex problems—to think through a situation, consider all the relevant factors, arrive at a viable solution, and communicate that solution to others (which is what we call persuasion). I believe, in most cases, the majority of those relevant factors involve logic—but not necessarily all of them. That's why a rational person must be able to use logic while also recognizing that logic might not always tell the whole story. Emotion is also a factor.

As *New York Times* columnist David Brooks observed, "cognitive scientists like Antonio Damasio showed us that emotion is not the opposite of reason; it's essential to reason. Emotions assign value to things. If you don't know what you want, you can't make good decisions. . . . Furthermore, emotions tell you what to pay attention to, care about and remember. It's hard to work through difficulty if your emotions aren't engaged. Information is plentiful, but motivation is scarce."

To understand Brooks's point, imagine that you've reached a crossroads in your career, as many of us do. One path is relatively safe but unexciting, while the other is exhilarating but fraught with risk. If you choose the second because you feel passionate about it, despite knowing the risks, that is a rational decision even though it's based to some extent on emotion. You've thought things through, examined the question from all angles, considered all the factors, and made your choice consciously and intentionally. For that matter, in this example, choosing the safer path would also be a rational decision, for exactly the same reasons.

All of that said, I do want to focus in this chapter primarily on logic. I've devoted ample space elsewhere, I believe, to nonlogic, and now it's time to give logic its due. Also, using nonlogic (illogic?) seems to come naturally to most people. It's using logic that requires some practice. But the first step is to understand what it is and how it works—or doesn't work, as the case may be.

A Few Words about Creativity and Imagination

Before we launch into our "cold" and "unfeeling" discussion of logic, however, let me say a few words about creativity and imagination—which I'm very much in favor of, by the way. I don't want to be accused, in this chapter or in general, of advocating for a Spock-like existence. In case you're not familiar with the original Star Trek series (and its various spin-offs), Dr. Spock was a character from the planet Vulcan, where people had long before learned to subordinate virtually every other cognitive activity to strict logical thinking. As a result, although Spock was highly intelligent, he often struggled to access or express his emotions or to "think outside the box," as we say nowadays—that is, to think creatively.

As I said, I'm a big proponent of creative thinking; I just don't believe it's antithetical to logical thinking. I'm not even convinced that it's something entirely different, a separate form of cognition. I believe imagination, at its best, begins with and flows from logic. No less an intellect than Albert Einstein called imagination "the highest form of research," while another creative genius, Walt Disney, put it this way: "First, think. Second, believe. Third, dream. And finally, dare." Note the order of things in that statement. "Dreaming" is what we normally think of as using our imagination. But Disney, whose imagination was probably as active as anyone's who ever lived, understood that productive dreaming starts with clear thinking.

So no, I'm not trying to stifle your imagination with all this talk of logic. Creativity, as such, is really beyond the purview of this book. But I do believe that, if you are a better thinker in general, you will ultimately be a more creative thinker. The skills you're learning here, about using your brain to solve problems, will serve you well as you are forced—in your other courses, in your profession, and in life—to "think outside the box." If you want to be creative, start with the basics: learning to think logically and employ reason. Creativity will follow naturally.

The Laws of Logic

Getting back to logic, then, scholars and philosophers have long acknowledged three age-old Laws of Logic: The Law of Identity, the Law of the Excluded Middle, and the Law of Noncontradiction.

The Law of Identity says that a thing is what is and not something else. Words have meaning, signifying specific things, based on tradition and general acceptance. It's true that word meanings evolve over time, along with our understanding of things. Technological advances also contribute to the evolution of language. For example, the word "hood" once meant a head covering and nothing more; now we also use it to describe the front part of a car—something that didn't exist when the word originated. At the same time, you can't just arbitrarily change definitions. You can't argue that dogs have retractable claws simply by calling a dog a cat. A cat is a cat and a dog is a dog. A thing is what it is.

The Law of the Excluded Middle says that, with most issues, there is really no middle ground—there is no such thing as neutral. If a student fails to graduate from high school, they didn't "sort of" graduate. Either they graduated or they didn't. If you put your house on the market, eventually you either you sell it or you don't. You can't "kind of" sell your house. Logic says that most things in the universe are like that: Either they are or they aren't. There's no "sort of."

Finally, the Law of Noncontradiction says that a statement cannot refute itself and still be true. For example, to say that "there is no such thing as absolute truth" is itself an absolute statement. If there really is no such thing as absolute truth, then that statement cannot be true, because the statement itself is absolute. And if absolute truth does exist, then obviously the statement is also false. Either way, it's illogical.

Making logic-based arguments, then, requires us to call things what they are, acknowledge that they either exist or do not exist, and avoid self-refuting statements. Such logic may not be the sole basis for effective arguments, but it's a great place to start.

Cogent versus Fallacious Logic

Of course, not all arguments are strictly logical. In this context, it's tempting to use words like "good" and "bad," but those terms imply moral judgments that I often find irrelevant and misleading. As I mentioned back at the beginning of this book, I had a couple of professors who believed that anything logical is therefore "good"—that is, moral and ethical—while anything not strictly logical is therefore "bad"—immoral and unethical. I just want to reiterate, before we go any further, that I don't agree with that point of view—and I don't think Aristotle would have agreed, either. As we've already seen, there are extremely valid and effective ways of making arguments that are not logical at all. That doesn't mean there's anything wrong with them.

Strictly in terms of logic, though, there are "good" logical arguments and "bad" logical arguments: arguments that work and arguments that don't; arguments that are supposed to be logical and actually are logical and arguments that are supposed to be logical but really aren't. We refer to the former as "cogent" or "valid" (depending on what kind of logic they use) and to the latter as "fallacious."

We'll get into cogent or valid logic a little later. In this section, I want to focus on fallacious logic—arguments that are presented as being logical but which, if we examine them closely, turn out not to be logical at all. We often say, of such arguments, that they "don't follow," which refers to a common metaphor comparing logic to a flight of stairs, each step following naturally from the one before. When that isn't the case—when the next step in the sequence is missing or out of place or somehow wrong—then the logic breaks down.

As I suggested above, fallacious logic is not necessarily wrong or immoral. In a sense, both pathos and ethos are logical fallacies. Just because something affects you emotionally doesn't mean it makes sense, and just because someone appears believable doesn't mean they're right. Yet, as we've already seen, those are powerful forms of persuasion. More to the point, perhaps, great arguers have often used logical fallacies intentionally in order to make their case—like Alexander Hamilton in Federalist Paper No. 1, for instance (which I'll come back to in a bit). I've always believed that the responsibility falls on the audience to evaluate an arguer's claims and determine if they're valid. That's one of the main reasons I'm telling you about these fallacies: so you can recognize them when they're being used against you in an argument. The other reason is so that you can use them, selectively, yourself.

Indeed, some logical fallacies are so common that we've given them names. What follows is by no means an exhaustive list, but I do want to talk about a few of the more common fallacies, in order to illustrate my point and so that you'll know them when you hear them.

Begging the question. This phrase is often misused. Usually, when someone says that such-and-such "begs the question," what they really mean is "raises the question": "The mayor's budget proposal begs the question of how the city will pay for these new programs." No, the mayor's proposal doesn't beg the question; it raises the question. That's something different altogether.

Truly begging the question means stating up front, as a fact, the very point one is supposedly arguing, or at least the point one ought to be arguing. For instance, when a politician says, "We all know that the current tax structure isn't working," and then goes on to outline a new tax plan, that is classic begging the question. "No," I want to say to that politician, "we don't all know that the current tax structure isn't working. Isn't that what you're supposed to be arguing? Why don't you try persuading me that what we're doing now is wrong, and then maybe I'll be inclined to listen to your solutions."

Obviously, my hypothetical politician doesn't want to do that. Instead, they want to take a logical shortcut, getting me to accept their premise without actually offering any real evidence, so they can then move on to what they see as the "important part" of their argument. And just as obviously, a lot of people fall for this: "Gee, I guess if everyone agrees, it must be true," they think to themselves. That's not logical. It's a fallacy (and perhaps, though not always, a lie as well).

Straw man. Another common fallacy is the "straw man," in which the arguer invents an imaginary enemy (a "straw man") to argue against. The arguer then claims that this imaginary enemy is saying all sorts of things that aren't true, as a way of making their own argument seem more reasonable and attractive. An example of this is when a politician says something like, "My opponents claim that this new proposal will drive up the deficit." (Sorry to keep picking on politicians. But, other than advertisers, they are the professional arguers we're most familiar with. They are also among the best professional arguers, or else they wouldn't be where they are.)

In some cases, it's the "opponents" who are imaginary; no one is actually out there saying this proposal would drive up the deficit. The arguer invented them in order to make themselves sound like the reasonable one compared to those non-existent nay-sayers. At other times, it's the supposed counter-argument that is the "straw man." There may be opponents to the proposal, but they're not making that specific claim. And sometimes it's both: neither the argument nor the opponents are real. The arguer made both of them up.

Clearly, it's not logical to rail against something nobody ever said. But portraying yourself as the voice of reason can be a very effective, ethos-invoking strategy.

Ad hominem. "Ad hominem" is a Latin phrase that means literally "against the person." In other words, in this fallacy, the arguer at some point stops attacking their opponent's ideas and starts attacking the opponent personally. That's not logical because, even if a person has character flaws—as we all do—that doesn't necessarily mean their ideas lack merit.

There is, to be sure, a very fine line here. Sometimes, a person's actions do affect their credibility. If someone is a known liar, then it makes sense to doubt what they say. At the same time, just because they lied before doesn't mean they're lying now. A true ad hominem argument usually becomes evident when the arguer completely abandons all attempts to engage with their opponent's ideas and instead spends all their time and energy attacking the opponent.

Note that, like the straw man fallacy, ad hominem arguments are ethos-based. Remember what we said about ethos in the last chapter: People are more likely to believe the argument if they trust the arguer. But the inverse is true, as well: People are less likely to believe the argument if they don't trust the arguer. Ad hominem attacks are all about undermining the audience's trust in the arguer, regardless of the substance of their arguments.

False dilemma. If you want people to do something they don't really want to do, a good strategy is to give them only one other option—something they REALLY don't want to do. Parents do this with their kids all the time: "That's fine. You don't have to eat your peas. You can just go to bed early." In most cases, that's not logical because there are usually more than two choices. (I'm not sure about the peas and bedtime.)

We either have to raise taxes or cut Social Security? Really? There aren't any other options, like, say, cutting other programs or decreasing waste? Yet it's an effective argument because people don't want to cut Social Security. They'll vote for higher taxes if you can convince them it's their only other choice. But of course, it usually isn't.

When I was growing up, back in the 1960s, I often saw bumper stickers that said, "America. Love it or leave it." Obviously, this was a response to the Vietnam War protests that were seen, by some, as being unpatriotic. And yet, the merits of that war aside, the bumper sticker represents a completely false dilemma. This IS America, where people are free to believe and say what they want. You can absolutely hate this country and/or its government and still stay here. Or you can love it and go elsewhere.

Band wagon. This is probably the fallacy young people are most familiar with, because they use it all the time on their parents. (See, parents aren't the only ones who can be manipulative.) "But mom, all my friends are going to the concert on Tuesday, even though it's a school night. Why can't I go?" Of course, the clichéd answer that parents typically give to this entreaty is, "If all your friends were jumping off a cliff, would you jump, too?" To which the honest answer, if you're a typical teenager, is "Yes, of course."

(I once tried the jump-off-a-cliff line on one of my sons. He said, "Sure, dad." I answered, "Really? You'd jump of a cliff?" To which he responded, "Of course. If all my friends jumped first, I'd land on a big pile of dead bodies and be just fine." Ah, the perils of raising smart kids.)

Advertisers use the bandwagon fallacy all the time. Their goal is to make people feel like there must be something wrong with them if they're not doing what everybody else is apparently doing—which is to say, what the advertiser wants them to do. When Toyota says that the Camry is "the number one selling car in America," what they're really saying is, "Everybody else drives a Camry. What the heck is wrong with you?"

What makes this illogical is the implication that, because the Camry is the best-selling car, it must naturally be the BEST car, which simply isn't true. Don't get me wrong. The Camry is an excellent car. But it's not the best car. The best cars cost $200,000 and up, and they're not exactly the best-sellers. Hardly anybody drives them, because no one can afford to.

Red herring. The final fallacy I'll mention in this chapter is the "red herring," which refers to an old trick escaped convicts used to use to throw the dogs off their trail: they'd drag a dead fish across the path, thus confusing the dogs and disguising their scent.

In argumentation, then, a "red herring" is a point that doesn't really have much to do with the subject of the argument, but which distracts the opposition (and/or the audience) and diverts their attention from the real issue. This is a standard tactic for people who are losing an argument—to deflect, to obfuscate, to raise tangential but irrelevant points. If you ever find yourself, in the middle of an argument, wondering "What the heck does that have to do with anything?", then your opponent has probably tried dragging the proverbial red herring across their trail.

On the one hand, these fallacies represent traps to watch out for in other people's arguments—but they are also tools for you to use in your own arguments. There's nothing inherently wrong with using a logical fallacy to make your point. The danger lies in your opponent's ability to recognize what you've done, point out that you're being illogical, and attack you for it—and rightly so. But to be very blunt, most people will never pick up on the fact that you've used a fallacy. They'll just accept what you've said at face value, which is why fallacies are so effective.

The Federalist Papers were a series of essays—op-ed pieces, really—written in 1787 and 1788 by Alexander Hamilton, James Madison, and John Jay, arguing that the United States should adopt the new Constitution that had recently been proposed. In the very first of those essays, Federalist No. 1, Hamilton begins by noting "an unequivocal experience of the inefficiency of the subsisting federal government." That's classic begging the question. Obviously there were plenty of people who didn't agree that the system was broken, or else Hamilton and his colleagues wouldn't have devoted so much effort to arguing that it was. He goes on to insist that the document in question "[comprehends] in its consequences nothing less than the existence of the Union," which is another way of saying that the people must adopt this new Constitution or cease to exist as a nation. That's a classic false dilemma. Then he attacks his opponents directly, calling them "a certain class of men [who] resist all changes which may hazard a diminution of their power"—in other words, accusing them of opposing the new Constitution only out of self-interest. That's a classic ad hominem argument.

Clearly, the Federalist Papers were effective, given that the citizens of the United States at the time did in fact approve the new Constitution. (And I'm glad they did.) How much that one op/ed piece, Hamilton's opening argument, had to do with the decision is hard to say. But it obviously didn't hurt anything, and most scholars regard it as a brilliant piece of persuasion, setting up the highly detailed and factual arguments that followed.

Hey, if it's good enough for Alexander Hamilton, it's good enough for me. I mean, the guy had a Broadway musical named after him. What greater endorsement can anyone receive?

Proof versus Probability

When arguments that are purportedly based on logic turn out actually to be logical, we say that they're "valid" or "cogent," depending on what kind of argument they are. That's because there are two types of logical reasoning: deductive reasoning, which we also call "proof," and inductive reasoning, also known as "probability." Both consist of premises followed by a conclusion but take different forms.

Premises and conclusions. All arguments, logical or not, are constructed of premises and conclusions. (If they're illogical, then either one or more of the premises are false or else the conclusion doesn't follow from the premises.) The word "conclusion," in this context, does not refer to the last paragraph of an essay; rather, it means what the writer has concluded or believes to be true based on the evidence. "Premises" are the pieces of evidence themselves, the reasons the writer believes whatever he or she believes.

Often, in a piece of argumentative writing, we lead with our "conclusion," which we call a thesis. Essentially, we're saying to the reader, "Here's what I believe, and here's why." (We may also repeat our thesis, or conclusion, at the end, as a way of reminding the reader what we set out to demonstrate.) But in classical argumentation, the premises come first, followed by the conclusion: A and B and C, therefore D. (If you've ever done mathematical proofs, you probably have some idea what I'm talking about, as they take a similar form.)

Deductive reasoning. Deductive arguments have exactly two premises, one pointing to something that is easily observable and the other invoking a universal truth.

For example, the classic deductive construction, also known as a syllogism, was given to us by Plato, who said:

> **Socrates is a man;**
> **All men are mortal;**
> **Therefore, Socrates is mortal.**

In other words, to translate Plato's syllogism into slightly more modern English (not that he spoke English at all), "Socrates is a human being; all human beings die; therefore, Socrates is going to die." The first premise is easily observable; presumably, anyone could look at Socrates and tell that he was a human being. The second is a universal truth: everybody dies.

We refer to this kind of argument as "proof" because, if both premises are true, and the conclusion follows from the premises, then it (the conclusion) MUST be true. If Socrates was a person, and everybody dies, then Socrates would eventually die (which, by the way, he did). Note, though, that the premise has to follow. If we say, "Socrates is a man, and all men are mortal, so therefore Socrates must love to watch football," that wouldn't be a valid argument. The conclusion doesn't follow from the premises.

That said, genuine deductive reasoning is actually pretty rare, for one obvious reason: How many universal truths can you come up with, even if we define "universal truth" broadly as something virtually all rational people believe? Let's see. Everybody dies. The sun comes up each morning (which is another way of saying that the Earth rotates on its axis). Can you think of any others? Any that are outside the realm of science or mathematics?

You see the problem. Without a "universal truth" there can be no deductive reasoning—and there aren't too many of those.

Unfortunately, fake (or invalid) deductive reasoning abounds. For example, all forms of prejudice are based on invalid deductive reasoning. You may remember studying in your history classes about the thousands of Irish immigrants coming to the United States in the early twentieth century as a result of the Great Potato Famine—and about the extreme discrimination they faced. Stores literally had signs in the windows proclaiming, "No Irish need apply," meaning they refused to hire anyone who was Irish.

Why not? Well, put into a syllogism, their reasoning went something like this: "Sean is Irish, and all Irish are a bunch of worthless bums, so therefore Sean must be a worthless bum." You can see how that takes the form of deductive reasoning—but you can probably also see the problem with it right away. It's not true because the second premise, the so-called "universal truth," is not in fact a universal truth. Remember, in order for the conclusion to be true—for the argument to constitute "proof"—both premises must be true. In this case, at least one of them clearly isn't, even assuming it's obvious that Sean is Irish. And please note, by the way, that technically speaking, it's only necessary to show that at least one Irish person is not a worthless bum in order for the argument to fall apart. Of course, the reality is that the Irish have no larger percentage of worthless bums than any other ethnic group, but that's beside the point, logically speaking. If the universal truth isn't universally true—if not ALL Irish are worthless bums—then the argument is not valid.

So genuine deductive arguments are pretty rare—which is the same as saying that actual proof of anything is pretty rare. "Proof" is a word we tend to throw around loosely, often confusing it with "evidence," which is not the same thing. I often see students write things like, "Statistics prove that . . . ." No, they don't. Statistics don't PROVE anything. They may show. They may suggest. They may indicate. They may provide strong evidence. But none of that is the same as actual proof, from a logical perspective.

In fact, there's an old saying in logic studies that "correlation does not prove causation." Note that "correlation" is a statistical term. It means that when we have A, we also tend to have B. "Causation" means that A *causes* B, which is something else entirely. But the key word in that phrase is "prove." Being able to demonstrate a strong statistical link between two phenomena may well indicate or suggest that one causes the other, perhaps even strongly. But, logically speaking, that's not the same as proof.

Back in the 1990s, when the tobacco industry was being grilled by Congress, CEOs of the tobacco companies were fond of saying, "It's never been proved that smoking tobacco causes lung cancer." Our general response, as members of the public, was to think to ourselves, "What a bunch of big, fat liars. How can they say such a thing?" But technically, they were correct. The cigarette-smoking-lung-cancer argument is not a deductive argument. It's not proof. (Which doesn't mean it's not a powerful and persuasive argument, as we'll see in a moment.)

Inductive reasoning. That brings us to the other type of logical reasoning, inductive reasoning, also known as probability. Unlike deductive arguments, inductive arguments are based on multiple premises—as many as possible. Basically, what inductive reasoning says is that the more premises you include—that is, the more evidence you can offer—the more likely your conclusion is to be true.

For obvious reasons, inductive arguments are much more common than deductive arguments. In fact, the vast majority of arguments that you will make in your career—and the vast majority of arguments you will face—will be inductive, not deductive. Most of the time, you won't be able to "prove" your point, in the technical sense, thereby putting an end to all argument; instead, you'll have to persuade your audience by amassing substantial evidence, countering the other side's evidence (more about that shortly), and using effective persuasive techniques, as discussed in the last chapter. On the bright side, your opponents probably won't be able to "prove" their point, either, which gives you a fighting chance in any argument. Usually, the winner of the argument comes down to who has done their homework and who can be most persuasive—although sometimes the evidence itself, even if not actual proof, is still overwhelming.

Consider the smoking-lung cancer argument we mentioned above. It's not proof, because there's no universal truth involved. Not everyone who smokes cigarettes develops lung cancer, and not all lung cancer victims smoke. But it is a very, very powerful inductive argument. (I'm certainly convinced.) To understand why, let's compare it to another argument based on correlation that, on the surface, may seem to have some similarities.

Suppose we found that, on the two nights of the week when the most ice cream is sold, the most violent crimes are committed. That's right: Friday and Saturday nights see the most ice cream sales, and they also see the most violent crimes. Can we therefore conclude that eating ice cream causes people to become violent?

Of course not. That sounds ridiculous on its very face. (Unless, maybe, we're talking about toddlers.) It's also not a cogent argument. But why? Not just because it sounds stupid. Correlation is not proof, but it is a form of evidence, a form that scientists and other researchers take very seriously. Often, a statistical correlation—when A is present, B tends to be as well—is the first clue that two things may indeed be connected, leading to further study. People didn't used to think smoking tobacco was harmful, until doctors started noticing that lots of people who smoked were coming down with lung cancer. People had no idea that eating too much red meat could cause high cholesterol, which could lead to heart problems, until researchers observed a correlation and began looking into it. Correlation is not something to be taken lightly.

So why doesn't the ice cream-violence argument have any merit? Because there's no other evidence to back it up. The fact that two things both happen a lot at about the same time may be a clue, but it doesn't automatically mean they're connected. To show that eating too much ice cream may cause people to become violent, you'd have to look at all the people who ate ice cream and see how many of them become violent. And you'd have to look at all the people who went to jail over the weekend for committing assaults and find out how many of them consumed ice cream. Chances are, both numbers would be very low.

You would also, to make a convincing argument that eating ice cream leads to violence, have to examine and eliminate other possible factors. Hmmm. Let's see. What other substance might people also consume on a Friday or Saturday night that might possibly lead them to commit violence? Alcohol, maybe? I bet if we looked at the numbers of people who got drunk and then became violent, and the numbers of people who became violent who were drunk beforehand, we'd find a much stronger correlation between alcohol and violence than between ice cream and violence. (Which is still not proof that drinking alcohol causes people to become violent, but it's enough evidence to suggest it's probably a factor.)

What makes the smoking-lung cancer argument so powerful, then, is the fact that it's backed up by so much evidence. Researchers have tracked the percentage of people who smoke and then develop lung cancer, and it's very high. They've looked at the people who have lung cancer, and a high percentage of them smoked cigarettes. They've also examined other possible factors—weight, diet, environment, and heredity. None has nearly as strong a correlation to lung cancer as smoking. That's a classic, winning inductive argument, based upon what they call in courtrooms "a preponderance of the evidence." (Note, by the way, that even though our legal system often uses the word "proof," most legal arguments, like most arguments in general, are really inductive, with the jury as the audience, listening to both sides and then making their decision based on which side they believe offered more evidence and made a more persuasive case.)

Let me conclude this section by giving you a little more concrete example of the kind of inductive argument you might be called upon to make in your professional life. I spent about ten years as an academic department chair, which is to say, a middle manager. As a middle manager, one of my primary responsibilities was to procure resources for my department—including personnel. For several of those years, the campus where I worked experienced astronomical growth, as much as twenty to twenty-two percent per year. That meant we were always having to hire new faculty members just to keep up with student demand for courses.

The college had a standard procedure for hiring new, full-time faculty. Each fall, the chairs would project their growth for the coming year and submit formal requests for new positions based on those projections. So, as Humanities chair, I might look at the numbers and calculate that I would need four new English professors and two new communication professors the following fall just to keep up with growth. Oh, and one of my art professors was retiring, so I needed to replace her, too. That meant I was asking for seven new faculty members for my department alone. Each of the other five chairs on campus did the same thing and submitted requests for their departments. Collectively, we might be asking for thirty new hires, overall—again, just to meet student demand.

Then, about a month later, the college administration would get back to us and say something like, "Okay, based on the budget, we can hire twelve new full-time faculty members for the entire campus." At that moment, it became my job to snag as many of those people as possible for my department—even as my colleagues, the other chairs, were all trying to do the same. I certainly wasn't going to get seven out of twelve, but I might get four or five if I could make a good enough argument. And it was clearly an inductive argument. There was no way to "prove" I needed an English professor more than the science chair needed a biologist; I had to make my case by citing evidence, mostly in the form of enrollment data (I won't bore you with the nuts and bolts here), and attempting to be more persuasive.

That was how the process worked all the way up to the final "horse-trading" session, where the department chairs sat around a conference table with the dean and made the final decision about who got how many new faculty. Frankly, I was pretty good at making those arguments (I'm a professional arguer, after all), so I was often more or less in the driver's seat. But there would often come a point when, looking at all the data, I had to acknowledge that the science department really did need a biologist more than I needed a fourth new English instructor. At other times, I might do some horse-trading: "Okay, you can have that position for a biologist this year, and I'll just use adjuncts to fill in for my retiring art teacher, but next year, I get that art teacher." Even if I'd already won the argument, I would make concessions (true concessions, not the fake concessions or acknowledgements we talked about in the last chapter) for the good of the campus. (That, by the way, is also a good example of going beyond logic—the data supporting my need for a new instructor—and using reason, factoring in abstractions like "the greater good.")

But all the way up to that point, my objective—indeed, my very job—was to win the argument and nab as many of those twelve positions as possible for my department. I attempted to do so by making the strongest inductive argument I could, pulling together as much solid evidence as possible to support my case. Those are the kinds of arguments that you, as professional, will most often be making, where neither side can "prove" anything. It will just come down to who has the best evidence and who can be more persuasive.

Case Study: The Traffic Ticket

To further illustrate the difference between deductive and inductive reasoning, and show how each can be used, let me tell you a story about a traffic ticket I received that I didn't deserve. (I know. Everybody says that. But in this case, it was true—and fortunately, I was able to prove it. And I mean literally prove it.)

A few years ago, I received an envelope in the mail from our local law enforcement agency. Inside was a citation for passing a school bus while it was stopped with its signal on—a serious (and expensive) offense. Also included in the envelope were two grainy photographs, taken by the bus's on-board cameras. One showed a vehicle—supposedly mine—passing the bus, and the second was an enlargement of the license plate on the offending vehicle. That was sufficient proof I had violated the law, right?

Not so fast.

At first, I was perplexed, not to mention dismayed. The vehicle in the photos certainly looked like mine, except that it seemed a little darker in color—although the quality of the image might account for that. But, according to the citation, the incident took place in a part of town several miles from my home that I almost never visit. I don't know anyone there, I don't shop there, I don't go to the doctor or dentist there. I've only been there once or twice in my life, and certainly not, as far as I could remember, anytime recently. Since my wife usually drives that vehicle, I wondered fleetingly if maybe she had been in that part of town. But no, I realized, looking at the date stamp on the photos. She had been in another state entirely on that day, visiting our daughter and her family.

Next, I went outside to see if the license plate in photograph matched mine. (No, I haven't memorized my plate numbers. Has anyone?) Again, it was close—except for the "3," which in the grainy photo looked more like an "8." I also noticed, as I looked at the back of my car, that the vehicle in the photo had a couple of stickers next to the license plate. As we never put stickers on our cars, I became convinced that the vehicle pictured was not mine.

But how to "prove" that in court in order to avoid the whopping fine? To be sure, I had formulated a fairly strong inductive argument, based on several pieces of evidence: The car in the photo appeared a shade darker than mine. That car had stickers on the back, while mine doesn't. The license plate number seemed to be different, if very close. I never visit that part of town. But was that enough to persuade the court? Were there any "facts" in my argument that couldn't be explained away by a good prosecutor? Did any of my evidence constitute "proof" that I had not committed this offense?

No, it didn't. What I had was probability, not proof. All things considered, it was unlikely that the car in the photo was mine. Yet, knowing bureaucracies, I doubted that would be enough to win the argument, convince the judge, and get out of the fine.

Then it hit me. I looked at the date again—and realized it was the day I had driven up to visit my parents, about two hours in the opposite direction. What's more, I remembered I had stopped for gas, and I was able to find a receipt dated that very day. In fact, the receipt was time-stamped within two minutes of the traffic citation. It also showed that I had purchased over twenty gallons of gas—and the only other vehicle we own is a small economy car with a twelve-gallon tank. So I could demonstrate, using her airline ticket, that my wife was out of town. I also could show, via the gas receipt, that the car and I were a hundred miles away when the supposed infraction took place. It could not possibly have been my car in that photo. I had proof positive.

That's deductive reasoning. If we put in the form of a syllogism, it would look something like this:

> **Rob's car was in City X on the date in question;**
> **An object can be in two places at the same time;**
> **Therefore, Rob did not pass a school bus in City Y on the date in question.**

The first premise is easily observable, based on the evidence—namely, the gas receipt. The second one is a universal truth. If both are true (which they are) and the conclusion follows naturally (which it does), then the conclusion MUST be true. That's proof.

Of course, as I noted above, we can't always make such compelling deductive arguments. It's actually pretty unusual to have such definitive proof. Most of the time, we're left with making the best, most persuasive inductive arguments we can, gathering as much evidence as possible in order to show that our conclusion is highly likely to be true. In this example, I had a reasonably compelling case, based on misidentification of the vehicle. It might have been enough—but there's no question that I was relieved to be able to actually prove my innocence.

And by the way, in case you're wondering, once I presented my evidence, the charges were dropped. You can't argue with proof.

Types of Evidence

Yes, absolute proof is nice. It's also rare; mostly, we're stuck with inductive arguments. How, then, can you make your case, if you can't literally "prove" it? What kinds of inductive evidence can help you persuade an audience?

I actually covered this topic in the last chapter, under the heading of paragraph development, and I don't see the need to rehash all of that here. You can go back and read it again, if it's not still fresh in your mind. For the purposes of this chapter, I'll just briefly recap the four main types of evidence:

Definition of terms. While definitions themselves are not necessarily evidence, *per se*, it is certainly true (as I noted before) that the person who defines the terms usually wins the argument. Remember the Law of Identity—that a thing is what it is and not something else. The catch is that we don't always agree about what things are. As an arguer, you're trying to define key terms in ways that are favorable to your argument. If your audience accepts your definitions, they have come a long way toward agreeing with your premise.

For example, if I'm arguing that childhood obesity is a problem in this country that needs to be addressed by parents, government authorities, and health professionals, then it is to my advantage to define "obesity" as broadly as possible. It's not just visibly overweight kids who are at risk, I might insist; it's also those we might just call "stocky," who otherwise seem healthy. Similarly, I probably want to define "childhood" in the broadest sense, too, incorporating not just young children and adolescents but also older teenagers. Such definitions serve to highlight the extent of the problem and thus help bolster my argument.

Factual information. Ideally, all arguments should be based primarily if not solely on facts. Unfortunately, that's not realistic, for the reasons we've discussed. Facts are often slippery things—subject to dispute and open to interpretation—so that even reasonable people operating in good faith may not be able to agree on just what the facts are. Plus, as we've learned, there are other means of persuasion that aren't necessarily factual but are quite effective, like pathos and ethos. But none of that means you shouldn't base your arguments on facts to the extent possible.

Factual information, as I noted in the last chapter, includes but is not limited to statistics—which, as we've seen, come with their own set of problems. Remember, correlation does not prove causation, which is another way of saying that statistics typically support inductive arguments, not deductive ones. Still, they can be powerful elements of inductive reasoning, strong pieces of evidence that go a long way toward persuading your audience.

Other types of facts include well-known information (such as that the world is round), things that are easily observable, and statements made by experts who have studied a topic and therefore know what they're talking about. Those aren't just expressions of opinion—we'll get to those in a moment—but rather factual statements based on years of study, research, and observation. For example, if a professional roofer that I trust, with twenty years of experience in the field, tells me that a shingle roof rarely lasts more than twenty years without developing problems, I take that to be a fact—and a good reason to have my 18-year-old shingles checked for leaks.

Expert testimony. Not everything experts say is factual just because they're experts. Facts are as elusive for them as they are for the rest of us. Nevertheless, things that experts have come to believe based on their experience, which we might call informed or educated opinions, are fair game as evidence. Someone who has studied American politics, for example, might opine that the new president's party will probably lose Congressional seats in the upcoming election, based on the fact that such losses are the norm. That's not a fact; the party might defy the odds that particular year, for whatever reason. But it is certainly an educated opinion, based on evidence, and therefore worth taking into account.

When you cite an expert's opinion in your argument, what you're basically saying is, "Hey, I'm not the only who thinks this way. This person who's a bona fide expert and who really knows what they're talking about is saying the same thing."

Sometimes called "appeal to authority," such a strategy makes your argument that much more persuasive, assuming your authority is an actual authority. Appealing to false authority—someone who claims to be an expert but isn't, or who is an expert but in a completely different field—can actually hurt your argument.

Examples and case studies. The last type of evidence you can use to support your argument involves citing examples. Again, I covered this topic pretty thoroughly in Chapter 9, but suffice it to say that illustrating your points by citing actual examples can have a profoundly positive impact on your audience, removing your argument from the realm of the theoretical and bringing it down to earth, in ways your readers or listeners can actually relate to. I can cite all the stats about childhood obesity that I want to, and there are many. But telling the story of one little boy who suffers from the disorder really makes my argument hit home.

Remember, too, that case studies are extended examples, often with a more clinical spin. Because of their length, they are usually reserved for much longer arguments, such as books, scholarly articles, and workshop presentations. (Note that I have used several case studies in this book.) Shorter arguments require shorter examples.

Finally, keep in mind that examples by themselves don't prove anything. In fact, by themselves, they might not even be particularly compelling pieces of evidence in an inductive argument. An opponent might accuse you of relying on "anecdotal evidence" if your examples seem dubious or you fail to place them in context. The key is to use examples in combination with other types of evidence, particularly statistics. Citing statistics can show the scope of the problem, while using an example gives it a human face.

Attacking Other People's Arguments

The final topic I want to cover in this chapter is what I called "refutation" in the last chapter—making your case by arguing directly against what the other side is saying. But first allow me to reiterate this key point: There will always be another side—a least one other side, and possibly many sides. Otherwise, there wouldn't be an argument. To win the argument, you must not only make the case for your thesis; you must also explain why your opponent's reasoning is not sound—that is, why they're wrong.

Excuse me if my language seems rather militant: "attacking" and "winning." Obviously, I use those terms metaphorically. But the truth is, in professional life, the whole point of arguing is to win. You want that hiring manager to invite you for an interview, not those other people who are also applying (i.e., making essentially the same argument you are). You want the company to eventually hire you instead of them. You want the client to purchase your goods or services, not your competitor's. You want the boss to adopt your proposal instead of a coworker's. You want to win. And that's good. It's necessary. It's the way careers are made, the way people advance in their chosen professions. There's nothing wrong with wanting to win an argument. At some point, you may need to back off, "take one for the team," or accede to the greater good. But up to that point, you're trying to win. That's what this book is all about: teaching you not only how to make arguments but how to win them.

To do that, you must first recognize and understand what your opposition is arguing. And you must be able to counter their arguments directly. We call this strategy "refutation," and it works a little differently depending on which type of argument you're facing.

Refuting deductive arguments. Deductive arguments are actually pretty easy to refute, assuming they're not true. If they're true, then there's nothing you can say. Remember, valid deductive arguments constitute proof. You can't argue with actual, honest-to-goodness proof.

The good news is that, as we've seen, legitimate deductive arguments are pretty rare, although fraudulent deductive reasoning abounds. Specifically, an argument that is framed as deductive—that essentially takes the form of a syllogism—is generally weakest in its second premise, the so-called "universal truth." It may also be vulnerable in its first premise, if what is supposedly "easily observable" isn't actually all that easy to observe. Or its conclusion may be flawed if it doesn't follow from the premises. But both of those are relatively rare. It's the supposed "universal truth" that usually isn't really universally true and therefore constitutes the weakest link in the logical chain.

Remember, too, what I pointed out above: To refute a statement that is alleged to be a universal truth, you don't even have to show that it's often or usually untrue. You just have to show is that it's not *always* true. A universal truth, by definition, is *always* true; otherwise, it's not *universal*. That's why faux deductive arguments are so easy to refute. The key is to recognize them for what they are, identify the two premises, and then show that the second premise is false. Voila! No more deductive argument.

Refuting inductive arguments. Inductive arguments are usually more difficult to refute just because they involve so many premises. There's so much information to deal with, and the arguer doesn't even have the burden of proof. They just have to show that their argument is more likely to be true than false—or, more to the point, that it's more likely to be true than your argument. That's what inductive arguments come down to: whose case is more likely to be true? Whose is more persuasive?

On the other hand, precisely because they have so many moving parts, inductive arguments present numerous opportunities for refutation. Think of an inductive argument as being like a fortress with multiple gates. You can decide which ones seem weakest and then direct your attacks accordingly.

The obvious place to start is by looking at the premises themselves. What evidence is your opponent offering in order to make their case? Identify each individual piece of evidence, then consider it separately. Is it true? Is it relevant? Is it complete, or does it leave out something important? Does it actually show what the arguer claims it shows? If you can demonstrate, in your own argument, that any single piece of evidence presented by your opponent fails to live up to those criteria—that is, it's irrelevant, incomplete, or downright false—then you have done great damage to their argument, if not blown it completely out of the water.

It is possible, perhaps, for someone to get one or two details wrong and still be correct, overall. But if you can show that they're wrong about anything, that automatically makes their argument appear less likely to be true—and it certainly makes it less persuasive. In the audience's mind, if your opponent is just flat wrong about anything in particular, then they might also be wrong about other things. Exploiting such weaknesses in your opponent's reasoning can go a long way toward helping you win the argument.

Another place an inductive argument might be weak is in its conclusion. Again, it's somewhat unlikely that a skilled arguer would assert a thesis that isn't actually supported by the evidence offered; it's much more likely, as noted above, that the evidence itself is flawed. But not all arguers are especially skilled, and many others intentionally try to get by with shoddy reasoning because they think their audience is stupid and won't be able to tell the difference. (Politicians, I'm looking at you.) In addition, because inductive arguments tend to involve so much evidence, they can become very complex. Even a relatively skilled arguer might well lose track of what they're trying to say and end up offering a conclusion that isn't really supported by the evidence. So it always pays to look closely at the conclusion and see if it follows from the premises.

A final strategy for attacking inductive arguments involves looking at what is NOT said—that is, significant pieces of information that are left out. (I alluded to this above when I mentioned that evidentiary points need to be *complete*.) It may well be that A, B, and C add up to D, as the arguer asserts—but if we add E into the equation, it totally changes the outcome. In that case, your job as an arguer is to bring up E, establish it as a viable point, and show how it negates the other side's argument.

Conclusion

In short, making effective arguments—usually in writing but sometime verbally—is a key component of any educated professional's job description. And in professional life, the whole point of making arguments is to win: to get people to do what you want them to do, such as hire you, buy your product or service, or adopt your proposal. There are many ways to make effective arguments, not all of them strictly logical. Emotional appeal and personal credibility can be powerful means of persuasion and should not be overlooked. But, in the long run, among professionals acting in good faith, winning arguments are almost always based primarily on logic—tempered with reason, which also takes emotional factors into account.

And don't forget, harking back to earlier chapters, that no matter how sound or persuasive your argument, it also has to be presented in a way that people can read and easily understand and that, ideally, they find engaging. That's why this book is about writing as well as thinking. You can be the greatest thinker in the world, yet if you can't communicate effectively, all your great ideas are basically useless.

REFERENCES

Brooks, David. "Students Learn from People They Love." *nytimes.com*. The New York Times. 17 January 2019.

Hamilton, Alexander. "Federalist Paper No. 1." *avalon.law.yale.edu*. *The Avalon Project*. 2008.

WRITING WITH SOURCES

First, a disclaimer: This chapter is NOT about using any particular documentation style, such as MLA, APA, Chicago Manual, or whatever. There are too many different styles for me to cover them all in one chapter, even if I were so inclined (which I'm not). Moreover, there are plenty of places you can go to learn how to use whatever documentation style is required, including online. (Again, check out the Purdue University Online Writing Lab, or the Purdue OWL.) And then there's the fact that many types of writing, such as newspaper stories or quarterly business reports, may not require formal documentation at all—but that doesn't mean, as a writer, you don't need to acknowledge your sources.

Indeed, when writers use information from other sources without letting readers know where they got it—well, we have a name for that. We call it plagiarism. The underlying principle here is that of *intellectual property*. A person's ideas and words belong to them—they are that person's property, in much the same way that their car or phone is their property. We can't just appropriate their words or ideas as our own. That's a form of stealing.

However, that doesn't mean we can't use them. The (mostly unwritten) rules of academic and professional writing say that we can borrow other people's ideas and even their words, provided we don't use too much and that, when we do, we acknowledge that we've done so and give appropriate credit—that is, identify our source. What constitutes "too much" may vary, based on the situation and applicable laws, but quoting a few sentences here, or referencing an idea or two there, is generally fine. Photocopying an entire book chapter to keep from having to buy the book, on the other hand, might be a problem.

In academic writing, the main way we acknowledge our sources is by using a documentation style such as the ones mentioned above. Typically, each academic discipline has its own favored style, so which one you're required to use will vary depending on whether you're writing for an English class, a psychology class, a history class, or what have you. For that matter, some of the hard sciences have their own styles that only they use. The key is to determine which style your professor wants you to use (they should tell you), find a good guide or manual that explains how to use that style, and then adhere to it meticulously.

Regardless of which documentation style you're following, though, or whether you're using any formal documentation style at all, there are some fundamental, time-honored strategies for using sources effectively—that is, integrating those sources into your writing in a way that makes sense, reads well, and is easy to follow. That's what this chapter is about.

Quoting

Perhaps, before we go on, we should briefly define the term "source." Basically, a source is where you got a piece of information, assuming it didn't come out of your own head. It could be an individual, an organization, or a government agency. It could come from a book, an article, a pamphlet, a Web site, a spreadsheet, a database, a speech, or a comment made during an interview. Nowadays, it could even come from a tweet or some other type of social media post. The point is that you're taking information or ideas that you discovered in the course of your research and using them to help you make your argument. Your "source" is the source of that information—that is, who said it or where you found it.

There are basically two ways to use information from a source: quoting and paraphrasing. We'll get to the second one later, but for now let's focus on the first. To quote means to take your source's exact words and insert them verbatim (that means "word for word") into your own sentence or paragraph, as if you were copying and pasting. Indeed, at times, you may actually BE copying and pasting, as you move back and forth on your computer screen from a source open in one window to a document open in another. But even if you're not literally copying and pasting, that's a pretty apt analogy. You're "copying" words from a source and "pasting" them into your own document.

Quoting is particularly effective when you borrow something a bona fide expert has said, whether fact or opinion, to back up a specific point in your argument. By quoting them, you're allowing those experts to speak for themselves while also speaking for you. There's great power in giving "witnesses" their own voice. Imagine a defense attorney saying to the jury, "Unfortunately, Mrs. Wilson isn't here today because she had a hair appointment, but let me tell you what she saw." No competent attorney would ever do that. Instead, they'd put Mrs. Wilson on the stand and let her tell the jury exactly what she saw, in her own words. That's because Mrs. Wilson is an expert—indeed, THE expert—on what she saw. And in the process of speaking for herself, she's also speaking on behalf of the defendant.

Please understand that quoting an expert in order to support your argument in no way diminishes you. It's not as though you're saying, "Well, gee, I'm so dumb, I have nothing to say, so I guess I'll just have to quote this other person instead." Not at all. The opposite is true: Quoting expert witnesses enhances your own credibility and makes you look smarter. Remember, an assertion on your part—that is, stating your own opinion—is not, in itself, an argument. It's merely an assertion. It doesn't become an argument until you support it with evidence, and one of the best ways to do that, as we learned in the last chapter, is by citing expert witnesses. You should be looking for opportunities to quote those witnesses whenever possible.

I say that because I'm constantly surprised at how sparingly my college students use quotes in their writing. Some of them don't use quotes at all, even in a research paper, where they're explicitly instructed to use quotes. I've never quite understood why that is, but I wonder if it has something to do with what I mentioned above—feeling like, if they use quotes, they're somehow admitting they don't know anything. The result, unfortunately, is that they miss out on countless opportunities to really drive home their arguments by quoting experts.

Quoting is so important, in fact, that one of the things you ought to be specifically looking for in your research is what I call "quotables"—things your sources have said that you can "borrow" by quoting. Quotables have three main characteristics. First, they make a point that you want to make. You read something and think to yourself, "Yeah, that's what I'm trying to say." Or else you see it in print and think, "Wow, that's good. I'm going to use that." Second, they do so in a way that you can't really improve upon. There's no need to rewrite the passage in order to clarify what the source is saying. It's already perfectly clear as it is. And third, quotables tend to be short—typically, a sentence or two, occasionally a little more, but often less. It's actually not unusual to quote parts of sentences or even brief, two- or three-word phrases.

Ultimately, it's up to you: You get to decide how much you want or need to quote in order to support your assertion—as long as you're not misquoting, taking the source's words out of context, or intentionally leaving out words in order to change the meaning. Those things are obviously dishonest and unethical. But beyond that, you get to choose where to begin quoting and where to stop quoting. The objective is to strengthen your argument by borrowing someone else's words, someone with more built-in credibility than you have. Quote as little or as much as you need to accomplish that.

Cropping and Crafting

The trick to quoting effectively is to incorporate those quotes as smoothly as possible into your own writing—to take the other person's words and weave them into your sentences and paragraphs in a way is highly readable and easy to understand. "Smoothness," in this context, means that quoted passages are compatible grammatically with the rest of the sentence or paragraph, that they make sense in context, and that there's not a jarring difference in the language or syntax. You don't want your reader to stumble over quotes because they seem out of place or don't quite fit.

There are two ways to attain that level of smoothness. The first is through a combination of cropping a quote to fit, as necessary, and then crafting your own sentences around it, which may require some trial and error. The second is using attributions, which I'll come back to a little later in this chapter. Right now, I want to explain what I mean by cropping and crafting.

For years, I struggled to teach students how to integrate quotes smoothly and effectively. Thanks to social media, I finally hit upon an analogy that seems to work. I now refer to that process as "cropping." We all know what cropping means when it comes to photographs. If you want to use a certain pic as your cover photo, but your ex is also in it, you can just crop them right out. (By the way, if you've been cropped out of someone else's cover photo, that might be a sign your relationship is not in a good place. Just saying.) If you want to post a photo of yourself and your two best friends on the beach, but there are too many dis-tractions in the background—lights or signs or buildings—you can just crop out those extraneous images. You want to be careful not to crop any of the important things—one of your friends or the beach itself—but you can certainly get rid of the stuff you don't need.

The same is true of other people's sentences when you quote. You can keep the parts you want and need while simply cutting or cropping out the parts you don't. You can also crop, as necessary, to make their words fit grammatically into your sentences. The quote below is from a sample college research paper in *The Bedford Handbook*, by Diana Hacker. In it, the writer cites several examples of horrible accidents that occurred because drivers were on their phones, such as this one:

> Early in November, two-year-old Morgan Pena was killed by a driver distracted by his cell phone. Morgan's mother, Patti Pena, reports that the driver "ran a stop sign at 45 mph, broadsided my vehicle and killed Morgan as she sat in her car seat."

Look for a moment just at the part of the sentence inside quotation marks. As you can see, it's not a complete sentence, in either sense of the word "complete." It's clearly not the mother's entire statement, and it's also not a complete sentence grammatically. It begins with the verb "ran," following the writer's subject, "driver." Obviously, in Pena's original sentence, she must have had her own subject. Why didn't the writer use it here? I don't know. I'm going to speculate that Pena used the guy's name—"Mr. So-and-so ran a stop sign"—and the writer of the research paper didn't want to go there. Nor was his name relevant. It had nothing to do with her point. So she just replaced it with her own subject—"the driver"—and started quoting with the verb, "ran."

That's a great example of cropping a sentence to fit grammatically. It's also a good example of the kind of smoothness I talked about above. Notice how seam-lessly those words borrowed from someone else, Patti Pena, fit into the writer's sentence. If it weren't for the quotation marks, you probably couldn't tell where the quote begins or ends. You might not even be able to tell it's a quote. Obviously, the writer has to use quotation marks to avoid plagiarism, because they are some-one else's words. But my point is that cropping allows the writer to integrate that passage into her sentence in a way that is not abrupt, confusing, or off-putting to the reader. In a word, it's smooth.

Of course, it isn't always possible to achieve that level of smoothness. Sometimes you're quoting someone with a Ph.D. from MIT who talks exactly like a person with a Ph.D. from MIT. Their words sound very different from your own, so it's obvious to readers, even without the required quotation marks, that you're quoting. (That's one way students get caught plagiarizing, sometimes.) But your goal is to work the quotes you need into your sentences as smoothly as possible, under the circumstances, and the key to that is cropping.

Or perhaps I should say, cropping AND CRAFTING. By crafting, I mean wording your own sentence so the passage you're quoting seems to fit naturally. Another useful term here might be "framing," placing the quote in context by putting words before or after (or both) that introduce it, explain it, and tie it into the rest of your sentence. That involves careful and deliberate "crafting" of language, in much the same way a woodworker painstakingly miters joints to make trim work appear seamless. Writers have an advantage over woodworkers, though, in that they can keep editing and revising until they get it just right.

Below is a sentence from an article I wrote a few years ago, in which I was talking about the Obama administration's "Complete College America" initiative. I wanted to make the point that President Obama himself was pushing this, so I scoured his speeches on the subject of education and found one in which he specifically talked about college completion. I ended up taking a couple of short passages from different parts of that speech and working them together into a sentence of my own, like so:

> President Obama himself has identified college completion as central to his economic agenda, calling education "the economic issue of our times" and vowing that America will once again "lead the world in college graduation rates by the end of this decade."

Once again, neither of those quotes constitutes a complete sentence. They're just short excerpts—in one case, only six words—cropped from much longer sentences. As I noted above, the two sentences weren't even together in the president's speech; they actually came several minutes apart. I'm the one who recognized they were related, put them together, and wove them into a single sentence by (a) cropping and (b) crafting my own language to frame the cropped passages effectively. That definitely required some trial and error on my part—writing the sentence in several different ways, quoting more or fewer of the president's words—before I settled on this final version, which I think works pretty well.

In closing this section, I should point out that it's not always necessary to crop a sentence. Just like a photograph, sometimes it fits just fine the way it is, and sometimes you want or need to use the whole thing. That's particularly true when the sentence is short to begin with, or when you're quoting two or three short sentences together. Here's another passage from my article on college completion, in which I quote former Education Secretary Arne Duncan bemoaning the state of American higher education:

> **"Other countries have passed us by," [Duncan] said. "They're outworking us. They're outcompeting us."**

Clearly, there's no cropping needed here. Duncan's sentences are short enough on their own, without any cutting on my part. Moreover, because they're so short, I couldn't really crop them without losing some of what he's saying. There isn't even much crafting required on my part. Those three short sentences fit into my paragraph just fine, without much help from me. It doesn't often work out that way; usually, you have to do some cropping and crafting. But occasionally you get lucky.

What About Long Quotes?

As we've learned, the most common way to quote is to take a short passage from one of your sources and work it into your own sentences and paragraphs by cropping and crafting as necessary. But that doesn't mean you can't sometimes quote longer passages, perhaps even an entire paragraph.

Such long quotes are relatively unusual, for the simple reason that, the longer the passage, the more likely you are to summarize all or part of it. (That's something we'll talk more about in a moment.) But there might be occasions—especially if you're writing something long and complex that uses multiple sources, like a research paper—when one of your sources has said something that really helps to support a particular point but just happens to be a little on the long side—maybe three or four sentences instead of one or two. In those cases, there's no need to shrug your shoulders and say, "Well, I guess I can't quote that. It's just too long." You absolutely can quote it, if you think you need to.

The exact format for inserting long quotes into your writing varies according to the documentation style you're using. (Each style even has its own definition of "long.") But most common styles call for "blocking off" a long quote, which means indenting on the left. Also, blocked off quotes don't usually require quotation marks, as those would be redundant. Blocking off a passage indicates that it's a direct quote, just like using quotation marks. You do one or the other, depending on the length of the quote and the rules of your documentation style. Be sure to consult your professor, or the professional standards for your discipline, to find out what style you're supposed to follow, then follow it as precisely as possible—with regard to long quotes and everything else.

Punctuating Quotes

Before I move on to paraphrasing, I want to address two other topics related to quoting: punctuating quotes and using attributions. The second of those actually relates to paraphrasing, too, if to a lesser extent, so it will provide a nice segue when we get to that point. Meanwhile, let's look at what types of punctuation are appropriate with quotes—other than the quotation marks themselves, which of course you have to use to indicate that the passage is quoted (unless you're blocking off) and thereby avoid plagiarism.

Many people seem to have the mistaken impression that a quoted passage must always be preceded by . . . something. A comma, a colon, a semicolon. Something. But that isn't necessarily the case. The truth is, when you quote, you use exactly the same punctuation you would use if you weren't quoting (except for the quotation marks, of course). For instance, if you wouldn't normally use a comma in a given sentence, don't throw one in just because you're quoting. It's true that quotes are often preceded by commas, but that's because we often introduce a quote using—wait for it—an *introductory* phrase, which is always followed by a comma. Consider, for example, the following sentence:

According to today's weather report, "A light, freezing rain will be followed by sleet and then snow."

The reason I put a comma after "report" is not because I'm about to quote the forecaster; it's because "According to today's weather report" is an introductory phrase, and we always put a comma after an introductory phrase.

Let's go back and look again at that sentence from Hacker's book:

Early in November, two-year-old Morgan Pena was killed by a driver distracted by his cell phone. Morgan's mother, Patti Pena, reports that the driver "ran a stop sign at 45 mph, broadsided my vehicle and killed Morgan as she sat in her car seat."

Did you notice that, in this example, there's no comma in front of the quoted passage—that is, in between "driver" and "ran"? That's because we wouldn't normally separate a subject and its verb with a comma, and there's no need to do it here just because the verb begins a quote. If we took out the quotation marks, we wouldn't need a comma there; adding the marks doesn't change anything. We use the same punctuation we would use if we weren't quoting, which in this case means no additional punctuation at all.

What about colons? When do we use those? Well, first, let's recognize the difference between a colon (:), which introduces things (like lists and quotes), and a semicolon (;), which performs other functions. It would be unusual for a semicolon to precede a quote, but colons often do—particularly when both the words that introduce the quote and the quote itself form grammatically complete sentences, as in this example:

The answer, as Smith points out, is obvious: "If the county commission wants to eliminate vandalism in West Bridge Park, it must increase police patrols in that area."

Obviously, the quote from Smith constitutes a complete sentence. But so does the passage that leads up to it, which has a subject ("answer") and a verb ("is") and expresses a complete or independent thought. That's when we use a colon instead of a comma—not just to introduce the quote but to separate complete sentences. (Otherwise, harking back to Chapter 6, we'd have a comma splice.)

One final piece of punctuation that we need to mention here is ellipses, the three dots (. . .). Used in a quote, ellipses indicate missing or omitted words. Most of the time, they aren't needed at the beginning or end of a quote, because it's already clear that something has been left out. In the Patti Pena quote above, for instance, where the writer begins with Patti's verb, we don't need ellipses to tell us words were omitted. It's pretty obvious.

We must use ellipses when we omit words from somewhere in the *middle* of the quote, because otherwise, the reader would have no way of knowing. As I explained above, when you quote, you can use what you need and leave out what you don't, as long as you're not misrepresenting your source. The passage you decide to quote may well contain words or phrases that are irrelevant or extraneous to your point; you can simply omit those and quote the rest. But when you cut words from the middle of a quote, in all fairness, you have to acknowledge that you've done so by inserting ellipses.

Here's another passage from my essay on college completion, in which I quote from a government report:

> The recently released Complete College Georgia calls for institutions to "increase the array of online programs . . . to enable all students . . . to effectively pursue college completion."

Like most bureaucratic writing, this report is a bit long winded (maybe more than a bit). The sentence I choose to quote contains a number of qualifiers and interrupters that are frankly, for my purposes, beside the point. They're extra—so I cut them out and substitute ellipses. However, I have an ethical obligation to let my readers know that I've cut words. Without the ellipses, it wouldn't necessarily be obvious. If for any reason readers don't quite trust me, or suspect that I'm misquoting, they're free to look up the report for themselves. What they'd find is that I just removed the fluff and kept the substance. But I fulfilled my obligation to let them know I had omitted words by putting ellipses in the appropriate places.

Using Attributions

As I suggested above, there are two ways to achieve smoothness when integrating quotes into a piece of writing: (a) cropping and crafting and (b) using attributions. Having covered the first of those pretty thoroughly, let's turn our attention now to the second.

"Attribution" is a journalistic term, referring to the way magazine and newspaper writers acknowledge their sources. Since those sorts of publications usually don't use footnotes, parenthetical citations, or works cited pages, journalists have to let us know in the text when they've quoted someone or otherwise used a source. They do so by "attributing" that information to the person or organization from whence it came. For instance, if a reporter is writing a story about a city council meeting, and quoting one of the council members, she might write something like, "According to Councilwoman Cynthia MacDonald," and then tell us what the Councilwoman said that is relevant to her story.

So why, you may be wondering, are attributions necessary if the writer is using a standard documentation style, as in the case of college research paper? Aren't formal citations sufficient to let readers know what sources the writer used? The answer is, technically, yes—but using attributions is still a good idea. In fact, I recommend that writers almost always (if not always) use attributions when quoting sources, even if they've acknowledged those sources more formally. That's because attributions actually accomplish three important things: They help us smooth out our writing, give us an opportunity to provide information about a source that doesn't appear anywhere else, and shorten parenthetical citations when the documentation style we're following calls for them.

The way attributions make our writing smoother is by eliminating what I call "naked quotes." A naked quote is one that is abrupt and unexpected; the reader is just reading along, minding their own business, when all of a sudden, BAM!—out of nowhere, there's a set of quotation marks. As readers, our natural tendency at that point is to stop and ask ourselves, "Where the heck did those come from?" Even if the sentence includes a formal citation at the end, we still have to stop and flip to the back of the essay or article to find out where it came from. That sort of thing takes time, interrupts the flow of ideas, and basically annoys the reader, especially when it happens often.

Fortunately, the problem is easily fixed simply by putting an attribution in front of the quotation marks: "According to Smith" or "As Smith has noted." Now the reader doesn't trip over the quote, wondering where it came from. It came from Smith. True, that doesn't actually tell us anymore than we might learn from seeing "Smith" in parentheses at the end of the quote. But the fact that it's at the beginning mitigates the abruptness of the quotation marks. We don't have to stop and wonder who said that. Smith said it.

Writers can even take this concept a step further, because attributions allow us to do more than just identify Smith as the person we're about to quote. We can also use attributions to tell the reader something about Smith that will make the quote more meaningful and, potentially, more persuasive. Remember why we're quoting Smith to begin with: because she's saying something that, theoretically at least, will help us make our case and ultimately win the argument. The quote, we believe, has persuasive value. But let's not forget that Smith herself might have some persuasive value, too.

For example, what if this Smith person we're quoting is actually Catherine Smith, Ph.D., who is a professor at Harvard University. Does the fact that she has a Ph.D.

make her any more believable? Does it have any persuasive value? Of course it does. And how about the fact that she teaches at one of the nation's leading research universities? Obviously, that has potential persuasive value, too. Both pieces of information make our readers at least slightly more likely to find her credible and therefore believe what she says. And where, by the way, do those pieces of information appear in our document? On the works cited page? No. We don't put things like degrees and academic titles on a works cited page. It just says, "Smith, Catherine" and then lists the title of her article, the name of the publication, and when it was published.

But what if we lead with something like this: "According to Dr. Catherine Smith, a researcher at Harvard University," and then quote her. Do you see the effect that might have? Not only are we avoiding naked quotes by using an attribution, but we're also leveraging that attribution to convey important information about our source that isn't included anywhere else. And we're putting that information right up front, before the reader even gets to the quote. Essentially, we're saying to the reader, "Hey, here's this person who is a recognized expert on the subject. Pay attention to what she says." That's potentially very powerful.

The last advantage of using attributions is that they can shorten (or, in some cases, even eliminate) parenthetical citations at the end of a sentence. Obviously, that only applies if the documentation style calls for parentheticals, but since several of the more common styles do, it can certainly be an issue. Because, let's be honest: Parentheses interrupt the reader. They can be annoying. And the longer they are, the more disruptive and annoying the become. Of course, if you have to use parentheses to cite your sources, then you have to use them. Otherwise, you might be guilty of plagiarism. At the same time, it's to your advantage as a writer to shorten parentheses or even eliminate them where possible because it makes your writing more readable. Attributions can help you accomplish that by communicating, in the sentence itself, the information that would otherwise go in parentheses at the end—usually, the source's name. Most documentation styles don't require writers to list that information twice—to put it in parentheses if it's already contained in the sentence.

That's why it's nearly always advisable to attribute when you quote. (I'm going to stop short of saying "always," because I'm sure there are exceptions. I just can't think of any right now.) It may also be a good idea to employ attributions when you paraphrase, but we'll get to that in a moment. Meanwhile, here's a short list of words and phrases you can use to attribute. There are actually far too many to list all of them here, but these should serve as examples. I've adopted the fictitious Dr. Smith as our source in order to demonstrate appropriate language:

According to Smith	Smith observes (that)
As Smith points out	Smith seems to believe
Smith notes	Smith reports
Smith argues	Smith found
Smith has observed	Smith says (or states)

The Art of the Paraphrase

Let's close this chapter by talking about the other way of using sources I mentioned at the beginning: paraphrasing. Unfortunately, this concept is frequently misunderstood. A few years ago, near the end of the semester, I walked into the library and saw one of my students sitting at a table with her laptop open and papers spread out around her. I assumed she was working on her research paper for my class, so I walked over to say hello and see how she was doing. As I approached, I noticed she had a small, paperback book in one hand. She kept glancing down at a sheaf of papers on the desk then flipping through the book as if looking up something.

"What are you doing?" I asked.

"I'm paraphrasing," she replied, holding up the paperback, which I saw was a copy of Roget's Thesaurus. She had found a passage in one of her sources that she wanted to use in her paper and was consulting the thesaurus in order to "paraphrase" it.

Clearly, that student grossly misunderstood what paraphrasing is and what purpose it serves. First of all, if a passage is so well stated that you need a thesaurus to figure out how to say it differently—well, just quote it. That's exactly the kind of thing you're looking to quote—one of those "quotables" I mentioned earlier. More to the point, paraphrasing does not mean simply using different words. To paraphrase means to take an idea or piece of information from a source but express it in your own words. When you quote, you borrow not only your source's ideas but also their words. When you paraphrase, you're still borrowing their ideas, but you supply your own words.

Why would you do that? We've already seen how effective quotes can be. So why would you use your own words when the source's words can be so powerful?

The fact is, quoting is not always possible—or at least, it's not always optimal. As much as you want to quote your sources, there will be times when it's simply more effective to paraphrase. Not everything you come across in your research, no matter how relevant, is actually "quotable." In fact, there are at least three common situations in which paraphrasing is preferable to quoting: when a passage is too long to quote, when it's not clearly written, and when it doesn't involve words.

We've already seen that it's okay to quote a long passage when necessary—but how long? How much do you really want to quote? Should you devote two or three paragraphs to a single point, when you have several other points to get to? Perhaps you should—but probably not. That's why, as I said earlier, the longer the passage, the more likely you are to summarize. That just makes sense. And summary is a form of paraphrase: You're borrowing ideas or information from a source and communicating them in your own words. An example would be a news article that you summarize in order to illustrate a particular point. You almost certainly don't need to quote the whole thing; you can just give the highlights, perhaps condensing a seven-hundred-word article into a couple of sentences for your purposes.

Of course, you may want to quote part of the article—maybe a short phrase here or a sentence there—and summarize the rest. That's actually pretty common. The point is that you're getting your information from a source—you weren't even aware of that event until you saw the article—but expressing at least some of it in your own words. That's a classic example of paraphrasing. (Please note that, whether you quote or not, you still have to cite your source, assuming you're using a standard academic documentation style. And even if you're not formally documenting sources, an attribution may well be called for—but more about that in a moment.)

A second good reason to paraphrase is that the passage simply isn't clear. Perhaps it's written in dense academic prose—not exactly uncommon in scholarly sources. Perhaps it's littered with jargon and technical terms. Maybe the writer is just a pompous know-it-all. Whatever the case, when you first encounter the passage, you suspect that it contains some useful information, but you can't quite make it out. So you read through it again . . . and again . . . and again, piecing it together like a puzzle. Maybe on the fourth or fifth reading, you finally comprehend what the writer is saying and think to yourself, "Yes, that's a good point. I believe I'll use it."

Well, by all means, use it—just don't quote it, because then the rest of us, your readers, will have to read it four or five times, too. You've already done the hard work of translating that passage into plain English, so please, give us the plain English version. Again, that's a classic example of paraphrasing: You're taking an idea you got from one of your sources and putting it in your own words, in this case because no one can understand the source's words.

The third situation that calls for paraphrasing is one people rarely consider, and that's when there are no words to quote—when all you have are numbers, taken from a chart or table or graph. Let's say, as a purely hypothetical example, that I'm making an argument in favor of stricter gun control laws. In my research I come across a pie chart, based on a FBI crime data, showing weapons commonly used in violent crimes. According to the chart, guns represent sixty-three percent, knives twenty-seven percent, and so on. (Again, I'm making up those numbers for the sake of my example; I have no idea what the true statistics are.) So in my essay, I say something like this: "According to FBI crime statistics, guns are used in sixty-three percent of all violent crimes." Am I quoting anyone? No. There was nothing to quote; I'm just pulling numbers off a chart. Once again, this is a classic paraphrase: I'm taking information I got from my source and couching it in my own words—this time because the source didn't use words.

What about attributions? Should you use those when you paraphrase? The answer is, sometimes—but sometimes not. Remember, you should (almost) always attribute when you quote, if for no other reason than to avoid naked quotes. But you don't have to worry about naked quotes when you paraphrase, because a paraphrase is not a quote. There are no quotation marks to potentially trip up the reader.

However, there are other good reasons to attribute paraphrased passages. First, as you may recall, attributions provide an opportunity to convey information about your source that doesn't appear anywhere else and that may well have persuasive value—and that's no less true for paraphrased passages than for quoted ones. Attributions also allow you to you identify your source, if you're not using formal documentation—and if you are using formal documentation, they can shorten your parentheses. You just have to judge, on a case by case basis, whether a paraphrased passage would benefit from an attribution or not.

The main take-away here, harking back to Chapter 8, is that in order to make a persuasive argument you have to cite evidence—much of which may come from your research, in the form of sources. When you use those sources in your writing, you must do so in a way that is clear, readable, and effective. The reader must be able to understand what point you're making, how the evidence you're citing relates to that point, and where you got your information—all without "stumbling" over clumsily inserted quotes or paraphrases.

Not all academic or professional arguments rely on "outside" sources, but many, perhaps most, do. In those cases, the success of your argument will likely hinge on how expertly you work those sources into your writing.

REFERENCES

Hacker, Diana. *The Bedford Handbook*. 7th ed. New York: Bedford St. Martins, 2005.
Jenkins, Rob. "Online Classes and College Completion." *chronicle.com. The Chronicle of Higher Education*. 13 March 2012.

WRITING EFFECTIVE E-MAILS

Everything I've said in this book about the importance of good writing, I believe, is true and has always been true. Indeed, I've been giving my students essentially the same advice since the mid-1980s. But over the last couple of decades, writing has become more ubiquitous in the workplace than ever before—and the ability to do it well has become correspondingly more important—all because of one simple, technological advancement that virtually everyone today takes for granted.

It's called e-mail.

Most people, I've observed, have a love–hate relationship with e-mail. They at least moderately dislike it and find it annoying, even stressful. In fact, when I talk to professionals about what stresses them out the most, many put e-mail high on the list—or, to be more specific, having to answer dozens or even hundreds of e-mails a day. And yet, nobody seems to know what we'd do without it. It has simply become part of our work-life landscape (and in many cases, our personal-life landscape, as well). I started my career in the days before everyone had e-mail, and I barely remember what it was like. As an administrator, especially, beginning in the mid-1990s, I started every day by checking e-mail, answering e-mails, and composing e-mails. How did I start my day back before e-mail? I honestly can't recall.

And yet, as much as people profess to dislike it, I don't see e-mail going away anytime soon. It's simply too convenient. It's a way to communicate quickly, essentially in real time, with people on the other side of the country—or the world. At the same time, e-mail is relatively unobtrusive and nondemanding, unlike a phone call or video conference. People can (theoretically) read e-mails at their leisure, and they can respond to them when they get around to it—or not respond at all. Text messaging and instant messaging have the same advantage, but the problem with those platforms is that they're not conducive to longer, more detailed communication. For that purpose, e-mail stands in a class by itself. (Of course, sometimes those e-mail communications can be TOO long and detailed, which is a problem I intend to address in this chapter.)

So perhaps the first rule of e-mail, before we get into the nuts and bolts, is this: Do not send an e-mail that does not need to be sent. Too often, as workers and especially as managers, we fall back on e-mail as an easy default position. Sending an e-mail makes us feel like we're "doing something," taking positive action. Too many times, though, all we're really doing is passing the buck, or kicking the can down the road, or simply trying to look busy. In my experience, a significant number of e-mails—maybe thirty or forty percent—accomplish nothing worthwhile and therefore didn't need to be sent. They just make work for whoever has to open and read them.

The second rule of e-mail follows naturally from the first, and that is you have no obligation to read every e-mail that comes across your inbox. Obviously, there are e-mails you definitely need to read (and probably respond to), such as from your boss or your professor, and those you can safely ignore, like solicitations and get-rich-quick schemes from faux Nigerian princes. The majority, however, fall somewhere in between. You have to decide whether or not to open them and then, after opening, respond. Here's a piece of advice that I've found works pretty well: If you're not sure whether or not to open an e-mail from someone, just sit on it for a couple of days. If it's important, they'll probably reach out to you again—and if not, then it probably wasn't important. Another strategy many of you probably use already is to have a separate e-mail address that you share only with people who are important either personally or professionally. But of course even that isn't foolproof.

For all those e-mails you DO have to answer, particularly in your professional life, there is this chapter. And, by the way, there's also the rest of this book. Because, when you write e-mails as part of your job, whether generating your own or responding to others, you are in fact *writing,* and all the principles of good writing that we've talked about apply. In fact, it's particularly vital that you write well in e-mail because many readers will "know" you only from your e-mails. Their perceptions of you as a professional—your intelligence, your competence, your level of education—will be based solely on what they read.

So don't fall into the trap of thinking you can get sloppy because "it's just an e-mail." That may be some of the most important writing you do, professionally speaking.

At the same time, e-mail as a genre does present some special challenges, because of the format and other considerations associated with the technology. In this chapter, I'd like to cover in detail what makes e-mail unique and how you can use it effectively, as a communicator and arguer.

(I'm not going to talk much about subject lines, because that's more of a marketing issue. When you're e-mailing people who are almost certainly going to open your e-mails anyway, then the trick to writing subject lines is to be concise and informative. Let them know, in as few words as possible, what the e-mail is about, so they can decide how to prioritize it. And if you're writing to someone who may or may not open your e-mail, and you want to use the subject line to entice them—well, like I said, that's a marketing issue, which is beyond the purview of this book.)

Length and Organization

One of the things that makes e-mail unique, as a form of business communication, is its format. It's strictly electronic, which means it has to be read on a screen. And one thing we know, based on more than a decade of research, is that people tend to comprehend less of what they read on a screen as opposed to on paper. As *Scientific American* magazine noted in 2013, that is simply a reality of our modern world, where many documents—not just e-mails—are now published online. But it is a reality that, as communicators, we must confront.

For me, the obvious conclusion is that when we write solely for the screen, as in the case of e-mail, we should be as brief as possible. We've all has the experience, as readers, of opening that interminably long e-mail and groaning inwardly (maybe outwardly, too). We don't want to read it, because we're busy and it's too long and no doubt boring (or so we assume); and even if we force ourselves to read, we're not really getting all of it. We're just skimming. Plus, we keep zoning out and trying to pull ourselves back on task. It's excruciating.

Why, as communicators, would we want to inflict that on others?

The short answer is, we shouldn't. If the first rule of e-mail is don't send one unless you need to, and the second is you don't have to read all your e-mails, then the third rule is this: When you do need to send an e-mail, keep it short. I recommend, generally speaking, that you limit your e-mails to not more than three hundred words—fewer, if possible. If you have more than three hundred words worth of information to convey, **put it an attachment** which recipients can then review at their leisure. Although e-mail is not as intrusive as a phone call, it still carries a sense of urgency, especially in a professional setting. If I receive a long e-mail in my business inbox, I not only feel like I need to read it, but I feel like I probably need to read it right then. That's where the stress comes in, because I might not have time to read the whole thing at that moment. But if the e-mail consists of just a few sentences along with an attachment, then I feel better about bookmarking it and coming back to it later. I'm also likely to read the attachment more closely than I would have read the long e-mail.

Much of the time, when we write long e-mails, we're just venting. Often what prompts us to drone on at such length is anger or frustration—and it's NEVER a good idea to send an e-mail written in anger or frustration. Sit down and write it, if you must. Sometimes expressing our emotions in writing can be a soothing, even cathartic experience. Just don't hit "send." (As an added precaution, you might want to leave the address line blank.) Then come back to the e-mail later, perhaps the next day, after you've had time to cool down and think rationally, and take out all the emotional language. Chances are, you can go from thousand words to three hundred just by doing that.

My argument for brevity applies at the paragraph level, too. Simply put, even a relatively short e-mail—two hundred words or less—should not take the form of a single, two-hundred-word paragraph. On the screen, that looks like a long e-mail. The reader's reaction will be much the same as if the e-mail itself were eight hundred or a thousand words. They'll assume it's dense, complex, and boring, and they won't want to read it. They'll resort to skimming and probably miss key points "buried" in the middle.

Take a look at this e-mail, for example:

Dear Department Members:

As you know, this Friday, January 5, marks the end of the fourth quarter as well as the end of the year for reporting purposes. That means all year-end reports must be submitted by next Friday, January 12. As always, I need those reports to be submitted to me, as attachments, via e-mail, no later than noon on Friday. Please be sure to follow the appropriate format for submitting year-end reports, which you can find on the company Web site if you're not familiar with it or need to brush up. If you have any questions, please let me know as soon as possible.

Sincerely,
Dr. Jones

That's only a little over hundred words, but do you see the problem? It looks and feels long. Important pieces of information get buried and might easily be missed. When are the reports due? What format do you need to follow? You have to read pretty closely if you want to pick up on those points, and that's not always easy, especially if your brain is already fried from reading seventy other e-mails.

Compare this rewrite:

Hello, all.

As you know, this Friday, January 5, marks the end of the fourth quarter as well as the end of the year for reporting purposes.

Please submit your year-end reports by noon next Friday, January 12. You can e-mail those to me as attachments.

Also, please be sure to follow the appropriate format for submitting year-end reports, which you can find on the company Web site.

If you have any questions, don't hesitate to let me know.

Thanks much,
Betty

Notice that I didn't change the wording of the e-mail very much, except to personalize it a bit, especially in the greeting and closing. (We'll talk about those a little later.) Mostly, what I did was break it up into several short paragraphs, instead of one long paragraph, making it infinitely more inviting and readable. Recipients don't take one look at it and think to themselves, "Oh, my gosh. This is going to be boring." Moreover, each key point—deadline, format—gets a paragraph of its own, which means readers are less likely to miss them.

I know this probably breaks all the rules of paragraphing you've ever learned, about length or number of sentences. Just remember: e-mail is a different animal, and we have to approach it differently. In e-mail, even more than other types of business writing, less really is more.

Tone

The word "tone," when applied to writing, is actually analogous, not literal. A tone is literally a sound, and of course the written word doesn't make a sound. People can only read what you're saying; they can't actually hear it, except perhaps in their head—in their "mind's ear," so to speak. And that presents a problem. When we listen to someone speak, we can infer a great deal from their tone of voice—whether they speak loudly or softly, talk fast or slow, emphasize or de-emphasize certain words. On top of that, if we're looking at them as they speak, we can factor in body language and facial expressions to get a sense of not just what they mean but how they mean it. Are they angry? Joking? Sarcastic? Frustrated? Based on how we perceive their tone, we might interpret their words differently.

Sarcasm is a perfect example. If my friend says, "I think the Braves are going to win the World Series this year," I might respond, "Yeah, right." Judging from my sarcastic tone, he deduces that I do not mean, "Yes, you are correct." Rather, what I'm saying is, "No way, dude" (and on top of that, "You're an idiot"). He understands that I'm being sarcastic because he can hear me (and probably see me, too). He knows not to take me literally or seriously.

When I'm writing, though, my readers can't rely on voice inflection or facial expressions to help them interpret what I'm saying. All they have are words on the page—or, in this case, the screen. Further complicating matters is the fact that, since readers can't literally hear what I'm saying, but can only "hear" me in their head, they are sometimes going to hear things I didn't say, or at least didn't intend. They're going to "hear"—that is, assume or imagine—a tone that really isn't there.

Thus we must take great care in all our professional communications to make sure we don't come across the wrong way—as angry or annoyed or frustrated. That's especially true in e-mail, because it's so short. In a longer piece of writing, a skilled writer might be able to project a specific tone on purpose in order to subtly manipulate the reader's emotions. We see this all the time in op-ed pieces, for example, where professional pundits try to move us to indignation, pity, or sadness in order to advance their argument. But an e-mail is not an op-ed piece, and most of us are not professionals. Even if that kind of emotional manipulation were appropriate in a piece of business communication (and it's not), most of us couldn't pull it off. We're better off not trying.

To be very specific, things like sarcasm do not translate well in e-mail—and even less so in shorter pieces of communication, such as text messages. Without voice inflection, facial expression, and body language to let readers know you're just kidding, they are at least somewhat likely to take you literally and end up believing the opposite of what you intended. Even people who know you well, who would probably "get" your sarcasm in person, might fail to pick up on it in an e-mail. That's why I say you're better off just leaving such attempts at levity out of your business e-mails altogether.

On the other hand, if you're too direct, people can assume you're angry when you're really not. I once worked for a campus leader who had a very, shall we say, blunt writing style. For the first several months, every time I got an e-mail from her, I thought she was mad at me. She sure *sounded* mad. Her sentences were short and clipped. Even requests came across like commands. I clearly remember wondering, after her latest e-mail, "What did I do now?" And it wasn't just me. Sometimes she'd send a group e-mail to several of us, and after reading it we'd wander out into the hallway and look at each other like, "What the heck is going on? Why is she so mad?"

The odd thing was, on several of those occasions, I happened to run into her a short time later, and she didn't seem upset at all. In person, she was perfectly pleasant. It took me about three months to realize that those "angry" e-mails weren't really angry. That was just the way she wrote. Her "tone" came across as angry, when clearly that wasn't what she intended.

In this example, we (the recipients of her e-mails) eventually figured it out and ultimately everybody got along just fine—in large part because we had a lot of face-to-face interaction. But, as we've seen, that isn't always the case. Often, in a professional setting, we're communicating via e-mail with people we don't know personally and might never even meet. Imagine if they thought we were mad at them all the time, and we didn't have those chance hallway encounters to straighten things out.

Of course it's good to be direct and to the point—especially in an e-mail, which is supposed to be short, anyway. At the same time, we must choose our words carefully so that people don't "hear" a tone we didn't intend. I refer to this as "softening." Consider these two examples:

Bob, see me in my office ASAP.
Please submit your reports to me by Friday. I need them no later than 3:00.
Thank you.

Can you see the problem? Sure, it's great to be concise, but these two e-mails go beyond that. They're terse. Clipped. They sound angry or at least short-tempered. (The "ASAP" acronym doesn't help matters, either.) The first one would leave most people sweating, feeling like they were being called in on the carpet and wondering what they'd done wrong. The second one seems to imply the unspoken phrase, "or else." I'm not sure that's the tone you want to take with the people who work for you, especially if they haven't done anything to deserve it.

Now compare these two edited versions:

Hi, Bob. Can you stop by my office when you get a chance? Thanks!
Please get me your reports by 3:00 on Friday so I have time to review them
before I have to submit them to the VP. I really appreciate it!

Do you see how I softened the language? In the first example, the command—"see me in my office"—becomes an invitation: "Can you stop by my office?" The unforgiving acronym "ASAP" gives way to the more congenial "when you get a chance"—without, I would argue, any watering down of the message or loss of urgency. (It's also not much longer; I only added a few words.) The second example adds a brief explanation (in addition to the "magic word," "please," which I've found works just as well with thiry-five-year-olds as it does with three-year-olds), essentially turning a demand for information into a request for help: "Hey, I've got a job to do here, too. I'd really appreciate your help." Most people (although, sadly, not all) respond well to such requests, whereas they are likely to bristle at demands.

Actually, what people respond to is being treated like human beings, not cogs in the wheel. And that means talking to them like human beings, acknowledging (however briefly) their feelings along with your shared humanity. For that reason, I often begin my e-mail messages with something mildly personal, like "I hope this finds you well" or "I hope your semester is off to a good start." If I happen to know more about the reader, I might even say "I hope you had a great vacation" or "I hope your daughter's soccer tournament went well this weekend." I've found that when I go out of my way to make e-mail exchanges a little more intimate, people are more likely to read those e-mails and get back to me, perhaps because they feel a human connection. We might be talking about business, but we're still two people having a conversation. Remember what said about a "conversational writing style" back in Chapter 8? The same principles apply to e-mail—only more so.

Finally, notice that in both of the examples above, the exclamation points at the end serve to lighten the mood. I'm not suggesting you start littering your e-mails with exclamation points, like a fourteen-year-old posting about the latest pop star, but occasional and selective use can be effective. In the absence of voice inflection and facial expressions to convey tone, sometimes punctuation can achieve much the same effect.

Greetings and Closings

Another way to improve your e-mails is by paying attention to the way you greet people and sign off. The greeting is the first thing recipients read, after the subject line; thus, it sets the tone for the entire e-mail. If you're overly formal, then then rest of the e-mail may seem dry, formal, and impersonal—assuming the reader even gets that far. If you're too friendly and not businesslike enough, then the reader might not take what you're saying seriously. The trick is to strike the right balance, based on the reader.

Audience analysis is no less important in an e-mail than in any other document. If anything, it's more important because e-mail is such a transactional form of writing, meaning it exists solely to create a transaction between writer and reader. Thus, e-mailers must take into account everything they know about the reader and tailor every aspect of their message—length, content, and tone—to appeal to that specific audience.

That certainly applies to greetings. Once you've identified your reader or readers, you should be able to begin your e-mail appropriately, based on your relationship. For example, you should probably address someone you don't know as "Mr.," "Ms.," or "Dr.," rather than using their first name, at least initially. (Pro tip: If there's a chance your recipient might be a "Dr.," find out for certain before you e-mail them. In my experience, people with doctorates really like to be addressed that way.)

Once you reach a certain level of familiarity, you can usually just greet people by their first name—unless they are significantly higher than you on the food chain, in which case you might still need to use their title (Mr., Ms., or Dr.) and last name. That often depends on the culture of your organization and profession—something you should be able to pick up on during your first few months on the job. (Pro tip #2: If you don't know a person well, but you're more or less on the same level, start by greeting them by title and last name, then sign off with your first name. That signals your desire to dispense with unnecessary formality. If they respond by addressing you by your first name, then you can do the same from then on.)

Along with names and titles, different greeting words signal varying levels of formality. The most formal option is "Dear" followed by the person's title and last name: "Dear Ms. Smith" or "Dear Dr. Jones." That construction should probably be used only in situations that are very formal indeed, such as legal notices. It isn't necessary in most business e-mails and can potentially have an off-putting effect. Using the person's first name along with "Dear" softens the greeting a bit while still maintaining some level of formality or professional distance: "Dear Bob" or "Dear Martha." And if you want to be more formal or respectful without sounding too much like a lawyer (even if you are a lawyer), you can leave off the "Dear" altogether and just greet them by title and last name ("Dr. Jones, . . .").

A much less formal greeting is "Hi" or "Hello" followed by the person's first name. That is perfectly acceptable, even advisable, in most professional e-mails between people who work together regularly and are therefore on a first-name basis. Just don't use "Hey," which seems too informal, not to mention somewhat demanding. ("Hey, you, fetch me a cup of coffee.") "S'up, bruh" is probably also inappropriate in a professional setting, if indeed it is appropriate anywhere outside of a Keanu Reeves movie.

Another word that can be used as a greeting is, ah, "Greetings," usually followed by an exclamation point. That may be appropriate if you're e-mailing a group of people you know fairly well, perhaps followed by "everyone." When I see it addressed to me, personally, I always feel like someone is trying to sell me something: "Greetings, Rob!" Sorry, but that's way too cheerful for me at 8:30 Monday morning.

Similar considerations should govern our closings. The most formal—the one that goes best with "Dear So-and-so"—is "Sincerely," followed by your full name and title. Just understand, when you do that, you're establishing a level of formality between you and the other person that will largely define your relationship, perhaps indefinitely. If that's what you want—and sometimes it is—then fine. Otherwise, you might prefer something a little friendlier and less formal, like "Regards" (or "Warmest regards") or "Best wishes" (or just "Best"), followed by your first name. If I'm asking for something in my e-mail, I often use "Thank you" (or just "Thanks") as a closing. Sometimes I'll say something like "Thanks, and best wishes, Rob," which seems to cover a lot of bases. (The cheesiest closing, in my personal opinion, is "Cheers!" which always sounds like the person has been watching too much Masterpiece Theatre. But there's nothing wrong with it, if that's the way you like to close.)

My main point is that we usually don't give much thought to our greetings and closings and the impact they have on the reader—the relationship they establish and the tone they set. I'm suggesting that we pay closer attention to those elements as part of a comprehensive strategy for writing better, more effective e-mails. It's far from an exact science, and you won't always get it right—at some point, you're probably going to refer to Dr. Smith as "Ms. Smith," thus incurring her undying wrath—but mostly you will.

Correctness and Appropriateness

As someone who has read tens of thousands of e-mails, I've observed that far too many people seem to think e-mails don't matter, that they aren't important, that e-mail itself is a kind of "throw-away" communication platform, like social media, where you can say more or less anything you want in any way that grabs you.

Nothing could be further from the truth. In fact, if you've learned anything at all from this book, I hope it's that there is no category of professional communication that fits the above description. It all matters—and in many cases, it matters very much. You have an obligation to make yourself as clear as possible to people who need to understand you, like your clients, your colleagues, and your supervisors. Moreover, fairly or unfairly, people will judge your competence, intelligence, and professionalism based at least in part on the way you write—and perhaps solely on that, if they've never met you in person. Most important, writing is one of the best vehicles we have—and in some cases, the only vehicle we have—for persuading people to do the things we want them to do, such as hire us, buy our product, or adopt our proposal.

That's no less true of e-mail than any other type of professional communication. If anything, it's even truer due to the ubiquitous nature of e-mail. It's the main way professionals communicate with each other in writing, and one of the main ways they communicate with each other, period. So of course it matters whether or not you write well in your e-mail correspondence. It may even matter more than just about anything else you do at work, despite the tedious and repetitive nature of checking and responding to e-mails. Don't let that lull you into thinking it's not important. It is important.

Hence, everything we've covered in this book applies to e-mail: the clear thinking that goes into making rational arguments, the engaging, conversational style that makes people want to read, the attention to grammar and diction that marks you as a serious professional. Specifically, the "five errors even the pros make" that I talked about back in Chapter 7 should be a cautionary tale for business e-mailers. I actually gleaned many of the examples I use in that chapter from e-mails I've read over the years. Such grammatical errors tend to be even more noticeable in an e-mail than in a report or proposal, because e-mails are relatively short. And if you think, just because you don't pay much attention to grammar, nobody else does either, then I'll just say that you are badly mistaken and probably embarrassing yourself without knowing it.

So what is the solution? I'll give you three words: proofread, proofread, PROOFREAD! I can't emphasize that enough. (Have I emphasized it enough?) Because your e-mails say so much about you, on so many levels, it is vitally important that you get them right as often as possible—especially when you're writing to people who have some control over your future, like a boss or client. I know you're busy, and e-mail often seems like just another chore. But take a few extra minutes, on those important e-mails, to read through them carefully and make sure you've said what you're trying to say, that it's clear, that it's reasonably concise while still conveying the appropriate tone (or at least not conveying an inappropriate tone), and that you haven't made any glaring grammatical errors that will cause readers to question your intelligence.

Beyond simply reading a document over and over obsessively, how do you proofread effectively? The problem is that even multiple readings might not catch every mistake; often we see what we think we wrote instead of what we actually wrote. (Ever done that? I have—and on at least one occasion, it ended up being extremely embarrassing. And I didn't even have autocorrect to blame.) The good news is that we can borrow some tried-and-true proofreading strategies from the pros. Obviously, these apply to more than just e-mail. You can use them on any piece of writing, and I recommend that you do. But I've saved them for this last chapter on e-mail because they're so important in this context:

- **Read backwards.** Instead of reading the text in the normal way, from beginning to end, start at the end and read backwards. That will force you to see what you actually wrote instead of what you think you wrote.

- **Read it aloud.** It's amazing what you can hear that you might never see on the page. I can't tell you how many times I've heard something I wrote spoken out loud and thought to myself, "Did I actually say that?" Either get somebody else to read it to you or record yourself reading it and play it back. Or, if nothing else, just read it aloud to yourself and listen carefully to what you're saying.

- **Find an "editing buddy."** My last piece of advice—and this really applies to all your writing, professional, academic, or personal—is to find a friend who is willing to read what you wrote and give you honest feedback. Perhaps you can agree to do the same for them. In the case of reports, proposals, or term papers, they might be commenting more on the ideas and strategies than on the finer points of grammar. But with a short e-mail, perhaps you can just get them to read through it and see if they notice any glaring errors.

In some ways, then, this last chapter is kind of the culmination of everything I've talked about in this book—taking all those principles of good thinking and good writing and applying them to the most common type of writing people do in the workplace. Of course, that doesn't mean those principles aren't just as important in other types of writing. They are, and in some cases even more so. But my overall goal, from the beginning, has been to help you improve your writing in practical ways that will benefit you professionally. I think becoming a better writer is a worthwhile pursuit for its own sake, but even if you don't believe that, or don't care, I hope you see that good writing is a vital skill that will help you to advance your career—a skill without which you may never become what you could have been. It's worth the effort to develop that skill. Not easy, but worth it.

I wish you the best in that lifelong endeavor and hope I have provided some small amount of encouragement along with much useful information. So long, and write well.

REFERENCE

Jabr, Ferris. "The Reading Brain in the Digital Age: The Science of Paper Versus Screens." *scientificamerican.com*. Scientific American. 11 April 2013.